Valerie Bothell

Joyful Stitch Combinations

350 Embroidery Designs

Seams & Samplers

C&T PUBLISHING

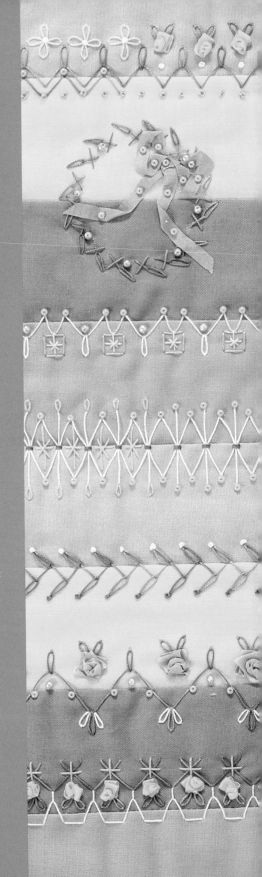

Text copyright © 2022 by Valerie Bothell

Photography and artwork copyright © 2022 by C&T Publishing, Inc.

Publisher: Amy Barrett-Daffin

Creative Director: Gailen Runge

Acquisitions Editor: Roxane Cerda

Managing Editor: Liz Aneloski

Editor: Karla Menaugh

Technical Editor: Debbie Rodgers

Cover/Book Designer: April Mostek

Production Coordinator: Zinnia Heinzmann

Production Editor: Jennifer Warren

Illustrator: Mary E. Flynn

Photo Assistant: Gabriel Martinez

Photography by Lauren Herberg and Diane Pedersen of C&T Publishing, Inc., unless otherwise noted

Published by C&T Publishing, Inc., P.O. Box 1456, Lafayette, CA 94549

Library of Congress Cataloging-in-Publication Data

Names: Bothell, Valerie, 1962- author.

Title: Joyful stitch combinations : 350 embroidery designs; seams & samplers / Valerie Bothell.

Description: Lafayette : C&T Publishing, [2022]

Identifiers: LCCN 2021053442 | ISBN 9781644031247 (trade paperback) | ISBN 9781644031254 (ebook)

Subjects: LCSH: Stitches (Sewing) | Embroidery.

Classification: LCC TT705 .B6625 2022 | DDC 746--dc23/eng/20211116

LC record available at https://lccn.loc.gov/2021053442

Printed in the USA

10 9 8 7 6 5 4 3 2 1

Dedication

This book is dedicated to Evelyn Hansen, my grandmother. Many summers were spent using her sewing machine to sew doll clothes, and she always believed in me. I love you, Grandma.

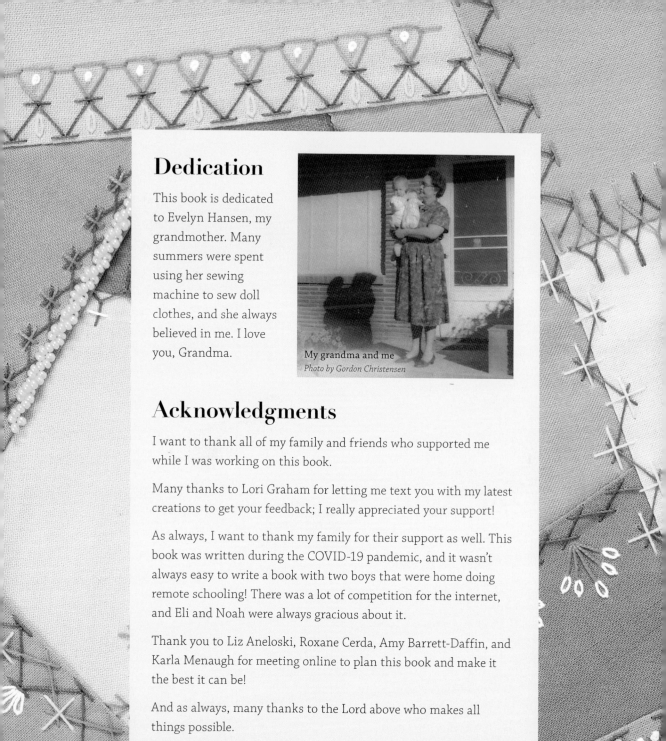

My grandma and me
Photo by Gordon Christensen

Acknowledgments

I want to thank all of my family and friends who supported me while I was working on this book.

Many thanks to Lori Graham for letting me text you with my latest creations to get your feedback; I really appreciated your support!

As always, I want to thank my family for their support as well. This book was written during the COVID-19 pandemic, and it wasn't always easy to write a book with two boys that were home doing remote schooling! There was a lot of competition for the internet, and Eli and Noah were always gracious about it.

Thank you to Liz Aneloski, Roxane Cerda, Amy Barrett-Daffin, and Karla Menaugh for meeting online to plan this book and make it the best it can be!

And as always, many thanks to the Lord above who makes all things possible.

Contents

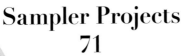

Sampler Projects 71

Hoop Holder
Crazy-Pieced Background

Flowers and Vines Sampler
Solid Fabric Background in a Hoop

76

78

Daffodil Sampler
Crazy-Pieced Background in a Hoop

71

74

Pansy Sampler
Strip-Pieced Background

Embroidery Stitch Reference 93

INTRODUCTION:
Welcome to *Joyful Stitch Combinations*

As I started thinking about what kind of art-work I wanted at the beginning of this book, I knew that I wanted you to feel welcome here. I wanted you to feel the joy that I do during my daily stitching and to get a sense of accomplishment every day for the beautiful things you are creating. I put myself in your place, as someone who wants to start some daily stitching. One of my favorite ways of making a sampler is to create a single crazy quilt block to display in a hoop. To me, these feel like the crazy quilter's version of a sampler, as you are trying different stitch combinations, either to practice or to stretch your imagination.

After piecing my blue crazy quilt block, I began looking through all of the new stitch combinations (next page). When starting your own project, you may refer to the Sampler Projects (page 71) to find 4 different ways to create a background for a sampler of your own. There are other sampler project ideas in the gallery (page 83), which include those stitched on crazy quilt blocks, solid fabric, traditional block patterns, or foundation strip piecing.

I am a firm believer in doing a little stitching every day. Most of these samplers are small and portable, and composed of 10–12 stitch combinations. So, if you do one stitch a day, you could complete a hoop or sampler in a couple of weeks! I've included instructions for an embroidered Hoop Holder (page 78) to help you keep your projects organized and to take with you wherever you go.

When I was done with my *Welcome* sampler, I was pleased with how it turned out. I found it so much fun to look through the stitch combinations and find the perfect embellishment for each seam in the sampler.

My best advice for using this book is to relax and enjoy the process of creating your own sampler!

—*Valerie Bothell*

350+ Stitch Combinations

This chapter contains 356 stitch combinations that are completely different from the ones in my last book, *Joyful Daily Stitching*. This time it was even more challenging to create new combinations, but it was so much fun! I kept a blank notebook on my desk, and when I would think of an idea, I would sketch it, hoping to make it come to life when I was ready to stitch.

Keep in mind that you can change the look of a stitch by using different colors of thread or using 2mm silk ribbon to do the stitch. Or you can add different beads, buttons, rose montée crystals, and glass or sequin flowers.

The instructions under each photo show the order in which you should stitch the combination. If a combination lists Featherstitch first, that is where I would start. Some stitches, such as the Circular Stitches, are organized by shape, but most are organized by the first stitch I used in the combination.

I hope that you can use these stitch combinations to make the sampler of your dreams, or—even better—use them to venture out and try some of your own stitch combinations.

This hoop was made using Essex linen-blend fabric (by Robert Kaufman Fabrics). The texture gives the project depth and really makes the addition of the silk thread and ribbon pop.

Backstitch + Straight Stitch

Backstitch + Lazy Daisy + French Knot

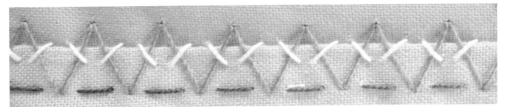

Backstitch + Straight Stitch

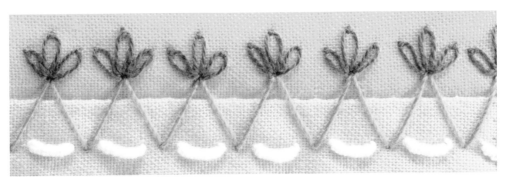

Backstitch + Lazy Daisy + Bullion Knots

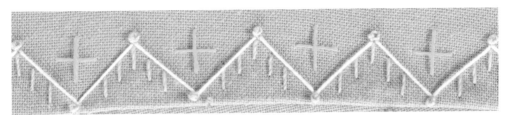

Backstitch + Cross-Stitch + Straight Stitch + French Knot

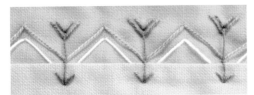

Backstitch + Fly Stitch + Straight Stitch

Backstitch + Fly Stitch + French Knot + Colonial Knot
Running Stitch Rose (4mm silk ribbon) + Lazy Daisy

Backstitch + Lazy Daisy + Straight Stitch

Backstitch + Lazy Daisy + Straight Stitch

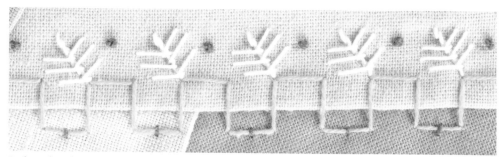

Backstitch + Fly Stitch + Straight Stitch + French Knot

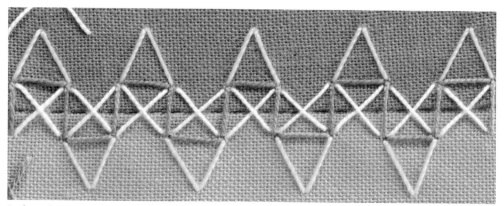

Backstitch + Cross-Stitch

Backstitch + Star Stitch

Backstitch + Cross-Stitch + Straight Stitch + Lazy Daisy + French Knot

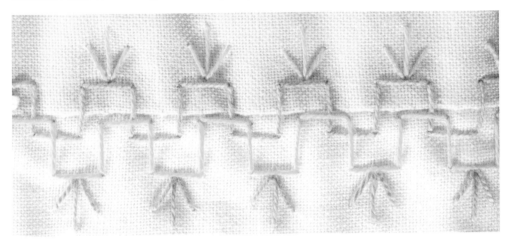

Backstitch + Straight Stitch

Backstitch + French Knot + Straight Stitch

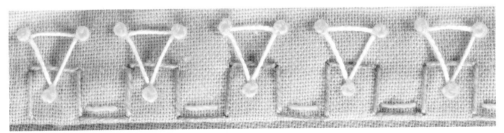

Backstitch + Straight Stitch + French Knot

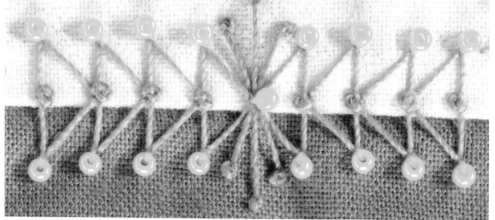

Backstitch + Pistil Stitch + French Knot + Seed Beads

Backstitch + Lazy Daisy + French Knot

Backstitch + Lazy Daisy + Seed Beads

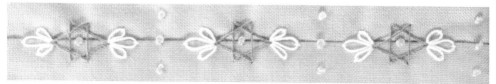

Backstitch + Lazy Daisy + French Knot

Backstitch + Straight Stitch + Seed Beads

Backstitch + Cross-Stitch

Backstitch + Straight Stitch + French Knot

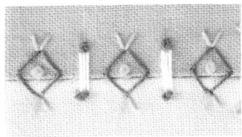

Backstitch + Straight Stitch + French Knot

Backstitch + Straight Stitch + Lazy Daisy + French Knot

Backstitch + Lazy Daisy + French Knot

Backstitch + Cross-Stitch + Lazy Daisy

Backstitch + Lazy Daisy + Seed Beads

Backstitch + Lazy Daisy + Straight Stitch

Backstitch + Star Stitch

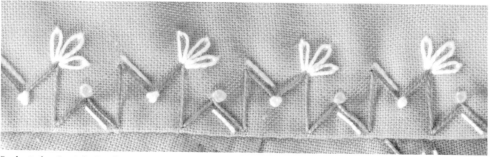

Backstitch + Straight Stitch + Lazy Daisy + French Knot

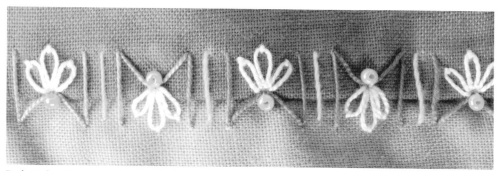

Backstitch + Straight Stitch + Lazy Daisy + Seed Beads

Blanket Stitch + French Knot + Lazy Daisy

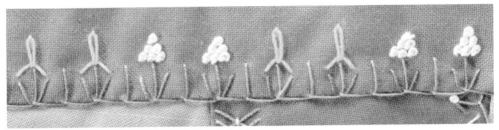

Blanket Stitch + Lazy Daisy + Straight Stitch + French Knot

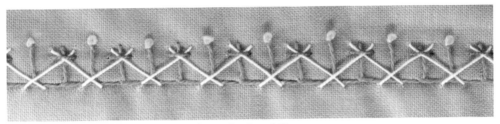

Blanket Stitch + Herringbone Stitch + Straight Stitch + French Knot

Blanket Stitch + Lazy Daisy + Fly Stitch

Blanket Stitch + Herringbone Stitch + Straight Stitch + Lazy Daisy

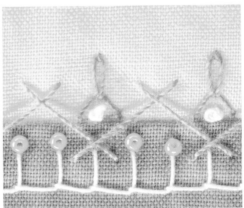

Blanket Stitch + Herringbone Stitch + Detached Wheat Ear Stitch + French Knot + Seed Beads

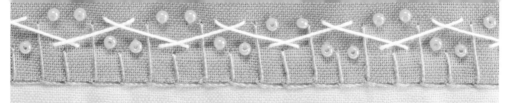

Blanket Stitch + Herringbone Stitch + Seed Beads

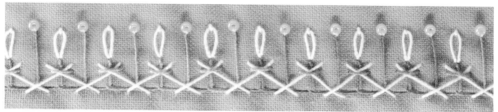

Blanket Stitch + Herringbone Stitch + Straight Stitch + Lazy Daisy + Seed Beads

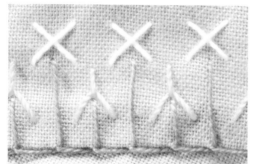

Blanket Stitch + Fly Stitch + Cross-Stitch

Blanket Stitch + Fly Stitch + French Knot + Ribbon Stitch (4mm silk ribbon)

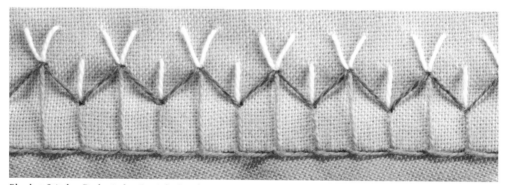

Blanket Stitch + Backstitch + Straight Stitch

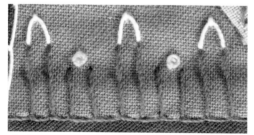

Blanket Stitch + Fly Stitch + French Knot

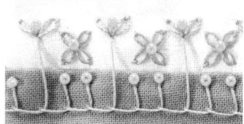

Blanket Stitch + Lazy Daisy + Seed Beads

Blanket Stitch (twice) + French Knot (twice)

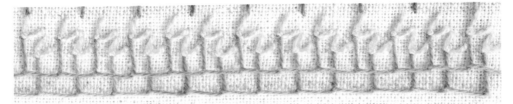

Blanket Stitch (twice) + Fly Stitch (twice)

Blanket Stitch (twice) + Lazy Daisy (twice)

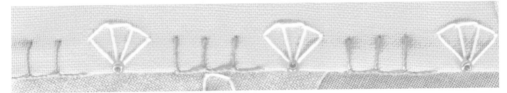

Detached Blanket Stitch + Blanket Stitch—Fan + Seed Beads

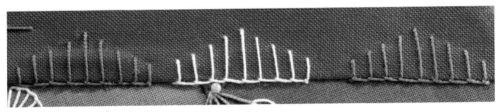

Detached Blanket Stitch

Detached Blanket Stitch + Star Stitch

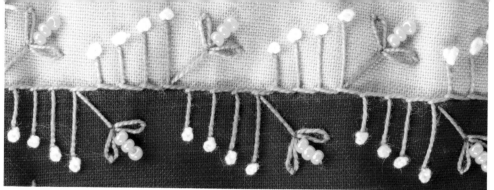

Blanket Stitch + Straight Stitch + Lazy Daisy + French Knot + Seed Beads

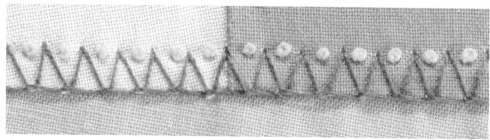

Blanket Stitch—Closed + French Knot

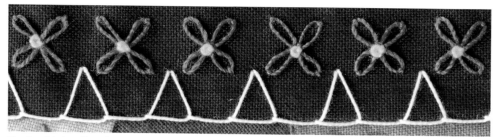

Blanket Stitch—Closed + Lazy Daisy + French Knot

Blanket Stitch—Closed + Lazy Daisy + French Knot

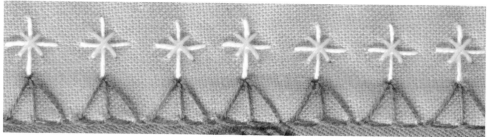

Blanket Stitch—Closed + Star Stitch

Blanket Stitch—Closed + Lazy Daisy + Straight Stitch + French Knot

Blanket Stitch + Lazy Daisy + Seed Beads

Blanket Stitch + Straight Stitch + Seed Beads

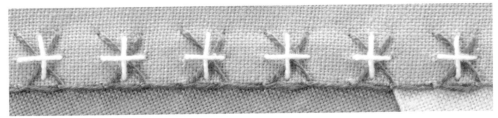

Blanket Stitch—Crossed + Cross-Stitch

Blanket Stitch—Crossed + Star Stitch

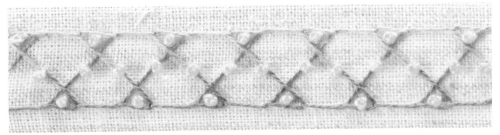

Blanket Stitch—Crossed (twice) + French Knot

Blanket Stitch—Crossed (twice) + Cross-Stitch

Blanket Stitch—Crossed (twice) + Cretan Stitch

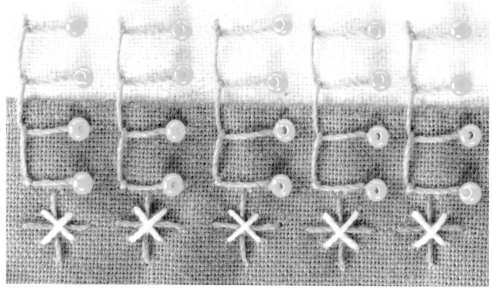

Blanket Stitch + Star Stitch + Seed Beads

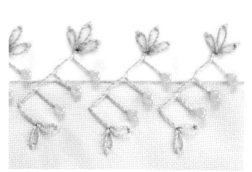

Blanket Stitch + Lazy Daisy + Seed Beads

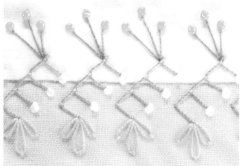

Blanket Stitch + Lazy Daisy + Straight Stitch + French Knot + Seed Beads

Blanket Stitch + Straight Stitch + Star Stitch

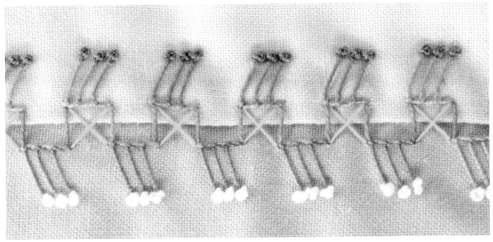

Detached Blanket Stitch + Straight Stitch + Cross-Stitch + French Knot

Blanket Stitch—Knotted + Lazy Daisy + Seed Beads

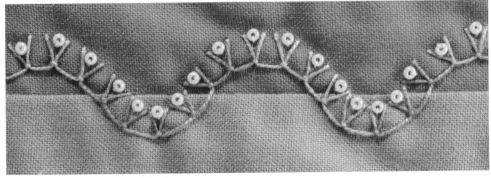

Blanket Stitch—Knotted + Seed Beads

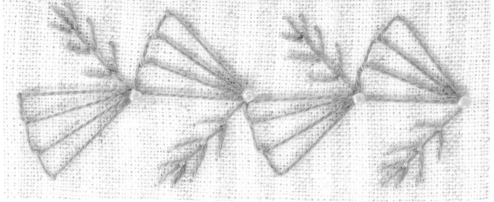

Blanket Stitch—Fan + Fly Stitch + Straight Stitch + Seed Beads

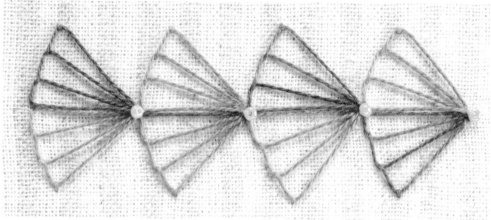

Blanket Stitch—Fan + Seed Beads

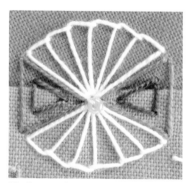

Blanket Stitch—Fan + Backstitch + Seed Bead

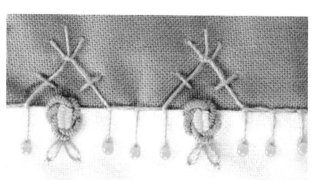

Blanket Stitch (done 2 different ways) + Straight Stitch + Bullion Rose + Lazy Daisy + Seed Beads

Bullion Knot rose + Lazy Daisy + Straight Stitch + Seed Beads

French Knot + Bullion Knot + Lazy Daisy

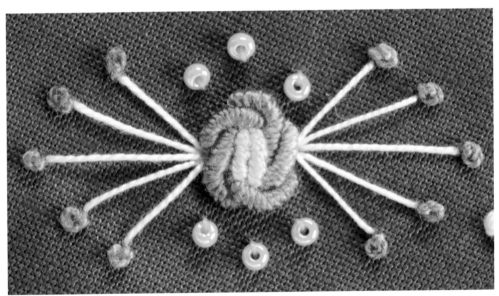

Bullion Knot rose + Straight Stitch + French Knot + Seed Beads

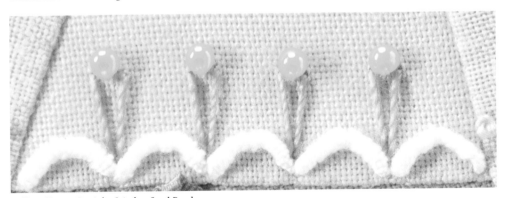

Bullion Knot + Straight Stitch + Seed Beads

Chain Stitch + French Knot

Chain Stitch + Fly Stitch + Lazy Daisy + French Knot

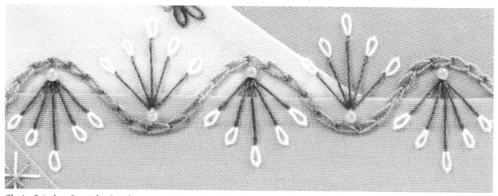

Chain Stitch + Straight Stitch + Lazy Daisy + Seed Beads

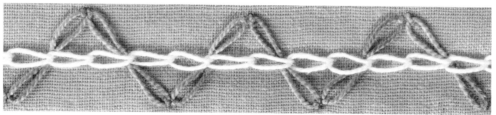

Chain Stitch (twice)

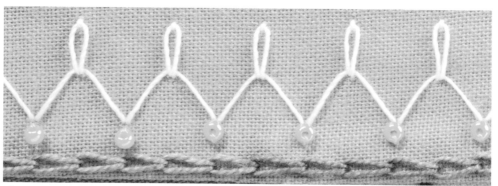

Chain Stitch + Detached Wheat Ear Stitch + Seed Beads

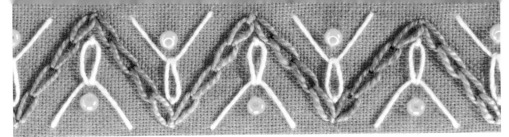

Chain Stitch + Detached Wheat Ear Stitch + Seed Beads

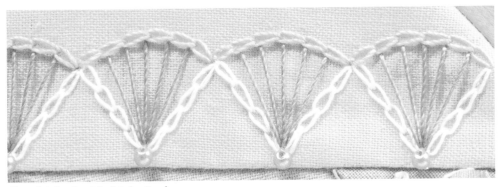

Chain Stitch + Straight Stitch + Pearls

Chain Stitch + Backstitch + Lazy Daisy + Seed Beads

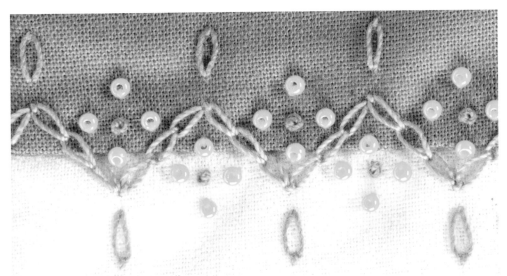

Chain Stitch + Lazy Daisy + Seed Beads + French Knot

Chain Stitch + Lazy Daisy + French Knot

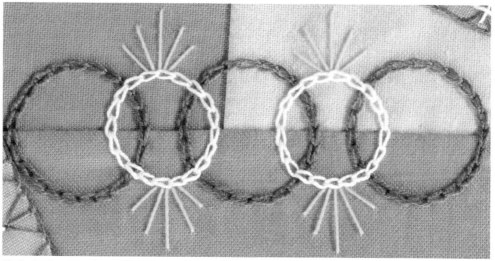

Chain Stitch + Straight Stitch

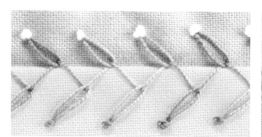

Chain Stitch—Feathered + French Knot

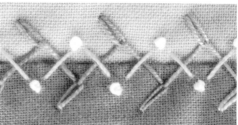

Chain Stitch—Feathered + Straight Stitch + French Knot

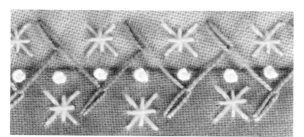

Chain Stitch—Feathered + French Knot + Star Stitch

Chain Stitch—Feathered + Straight Stitch + Pearls + Silk Ribbon Bow (4mm silk ribbon; Couched with Seed Beads)

Chevron Stitch + French Knot

Chevron Stitch + Lazy Daisy + Seed Beads

Chevron Stitch + Lazy Daisy

Chevron Stitch + Blanket Stitch—Fan + Seed Beads

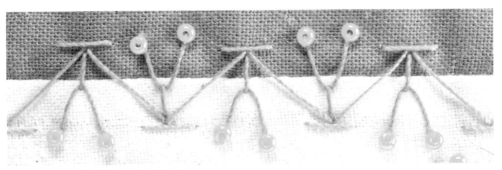

Chevron Stitch + Fly Stitch + Seed Beads

Chevron Stitch + Fly Stitch + Lazy Daisy

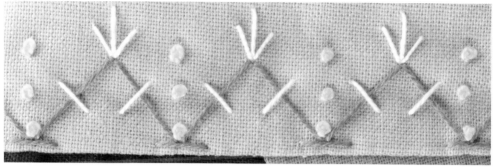

Chevron Stitch—Detached + Straight Stitch + French Knots

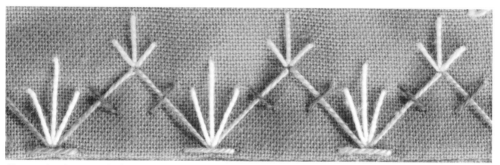

Chevron Stitch—Detached + Straight Stitch

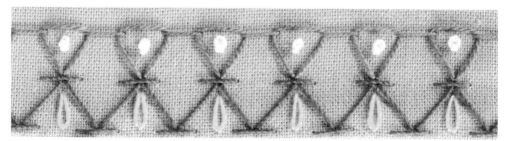

Chevron Stitch + Straight Stitch + thread laced through Straight Stitch + Lazy Daisy + French Knot

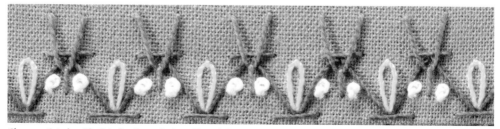

Chevron Stitch + Fly Stitch + Lazy Daisy + French Knot

Chevron Stitch + Detached Wheat Ear Stitch

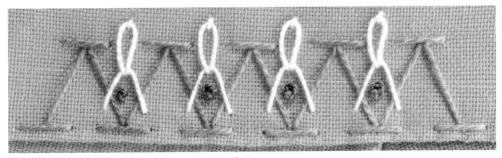

Chevron Stitch + Detached Wheat Ear Stitch + French Knot

Chevron Stitch + Chain Stitch + French Knot

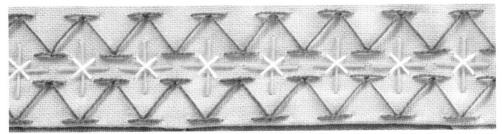

Chevron Stitch (twice) + Star Stitch

Chevron Stitch (twice) + Cross-Stitch

Chevron Stitch (twice) + Lazy Daisy

Chevron Stitch (twice) + Fly Stitch

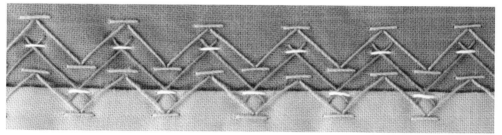

Chevron Stitch (twice) + Herringbone Stitch + Straight Stitch

Chevron Stitch + Herringbone Stitch + Cross-Stitch + Lazy Daisy

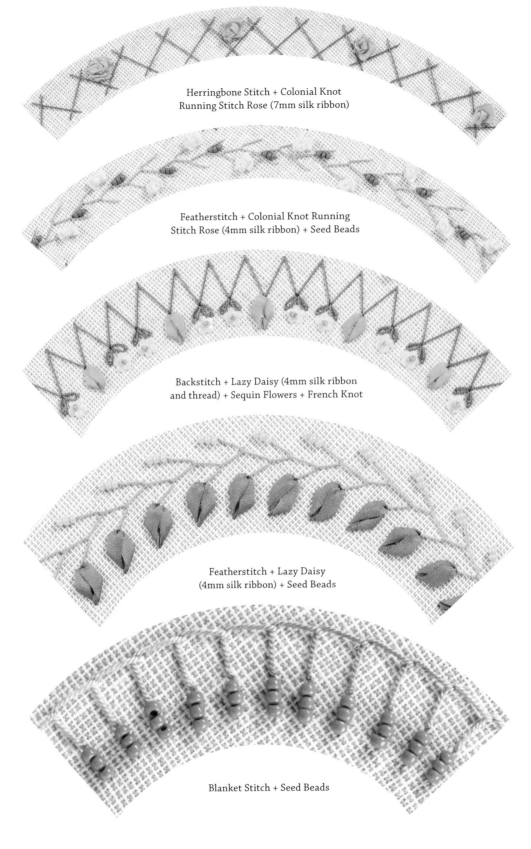

Herringbone Stitch + Colonial Knot
Running Stitch Rose (7mm silk ribbon)

Featherstitch + Colonial Knot Running
Stitch Rose (4mm silk ribbon) + Seed Beads

Backstitch + Lazy Daisy (4mm silk ribbon
and thread) + Sequin Flowers + French Knot

Featherstitch + Lazy Daisy
(4mm silk ribbon) + Seed Beads

Blanket Stitch + Seed Beads

Featherstitch + French Knot + Ribbon Stitch
(7mm silk ribbon) + Seed Beads

Featherstitch + Lazy Daisy (4mm silk
ribbon and thread) + French Knot

Featherstitch + Ribbon Stitch on the left side
of the ribbon (7mm silk ribbon) + Lazy Daisy
(4mm silk ribbon and thread) + Seed Beads

Cretan Stitch + Cross-Stitch

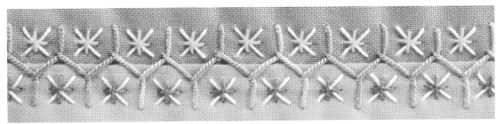

Cretan Stitch + Star Stitch

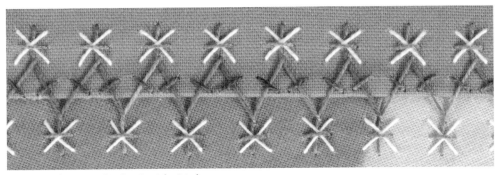

Cretan Stitch + Cross-Stitch + Straight Stitch

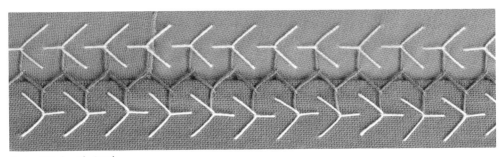

Cretan Stitch + Fly Stitch

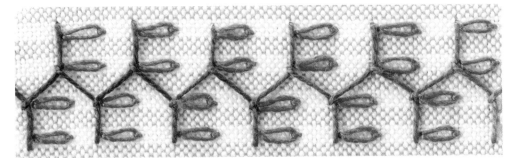

Cretan Stitch + Lazy Daisy

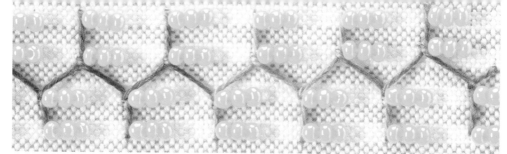

Cretan Stitch + Seed Beads

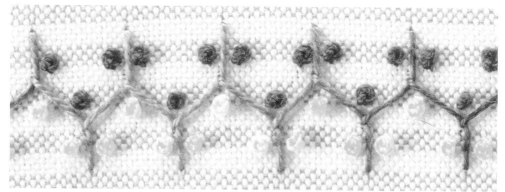

Cretan Stitch + French Knot

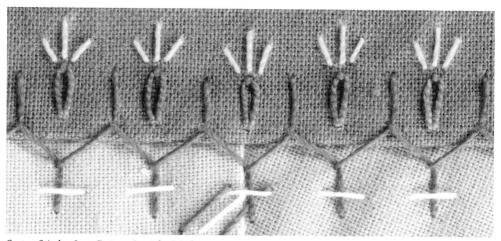

Cretan Stitch + Lazy Daisy + Straight Stitch

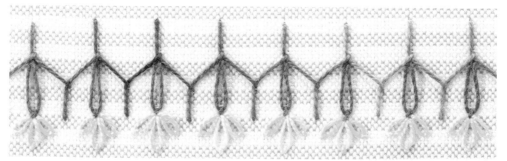

Cretan Stitch + Lazy Daisy

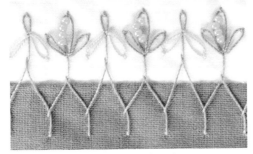

Cretan Stich + Lazy Daisy + Seed Beads

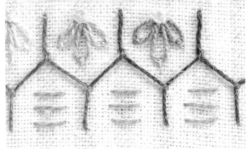

Cretan Stitch + Straight Stitch + Lazy Daisy + French Knot

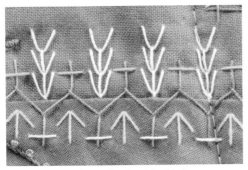

Cretan Stitch + Fly Stitch + Straight Stitch

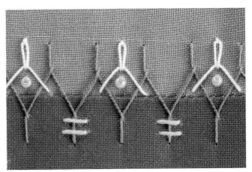

Cretan Stitch + Detached Wheat Ear Stitch + Straight Stitch + Seed Beads

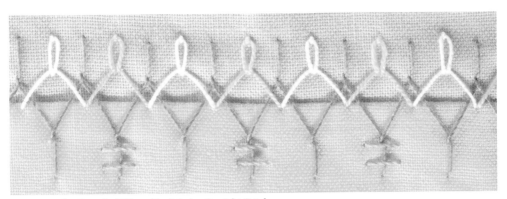

Cretan Stitch + Detached Wheat Ear Stitch + Straight Stitch

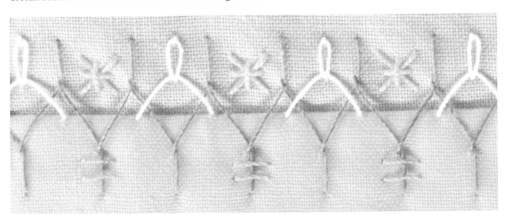

Cretan Stitch + Detached Wheat Ear Stitch + Star Stitch + Straight Stitch

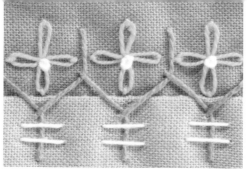

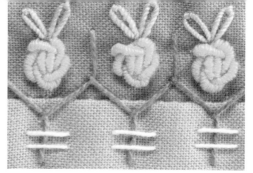

Cretan Stitch + Lazy Daisy + Straight Stitch + French Knot

Cretan Stitch + Bullion Knot rose + Lazy Daisy + Straight Stitch

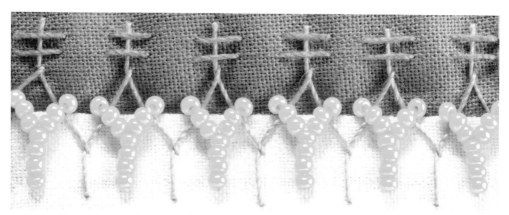

Cretan Stitch + Straight Stitch + Fly Stitch—Beaded

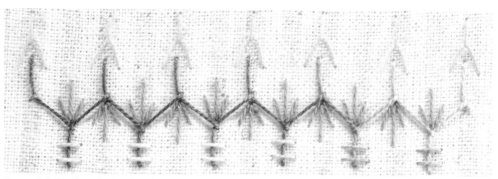

Cretan Stitch + Straight Stitch + Fly Stitch

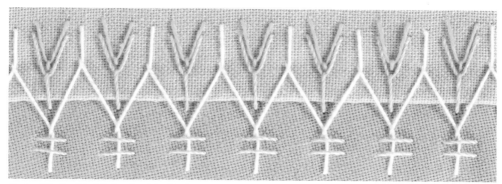

Cretan Stitch + Fly Stitch + Straight Stitch

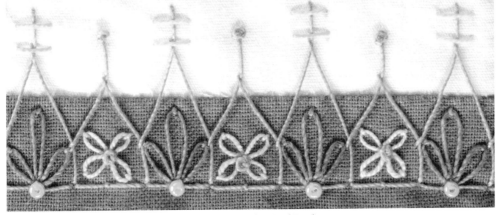

Cretan Stitch + Lazy Daisy + French Knot + Straight Stitch + Seed Beads

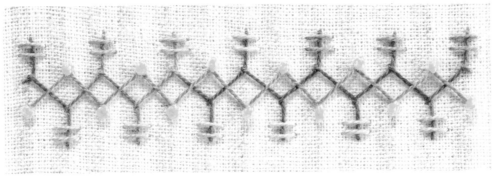

Cretan Stitch + Backstitch + French Knot + Straight Stitch

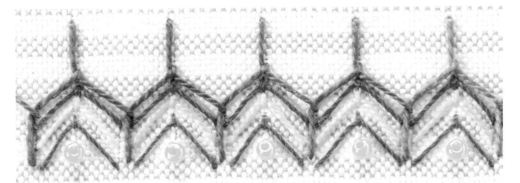

Cretan Stitch + Fly Stitch + Seed Beads

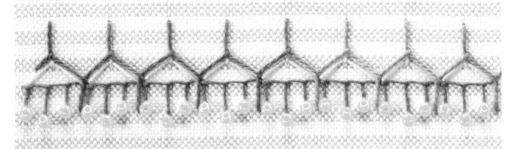

Cretan Stitch + Fly Stitch + Detached Blanket Stitch + Seed Beads

Cretan Stitch + Star Stitch + Fly Stitch + Seed Beads

Cretan Stitch + Cretan Stitch—Detached + Fly Stitch (hearts)

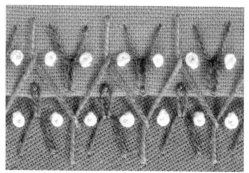

Cretan Stitch + Detached Wheat Ear Stitch + French Knot

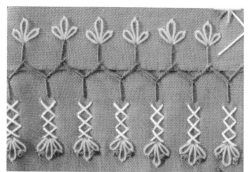

Cretan Stitch + Cross-Stitch + Lazy Daisy + French Knot

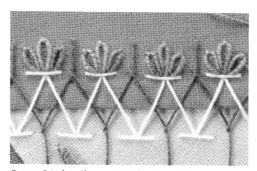

Cretan Stitch + Chevron Stitch + Lazy Daisy

Cretan Stitch—Detached + Lazy Daisy + Seed Beads

Cross-Stitch + Straight Stitch + Bullion Knot

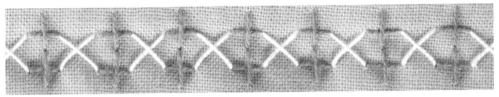

Cross-Stitch

Cross-Stitch (Couched) + French Knot

Cross-Stitch (Couched) + Lazy Daisy + French Knot

Cross-Stitch (Couched with Cross-Stitch) + Lazy Daisy

Cross-Stitch (Couched with Cross-Stitch) + Backstitch

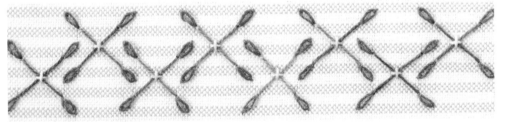

Cross-Stitch (Couched with Cross-Stitch) + Lazy Daisy

Cross-Stitch + Star Stitch + Straight Stitch

Cross-Stitch + Straight Stitch + French Knot

Cross-Stitch + Straight Stitch

Cross-Stitch + Straight Stitch

Cross-Stitch + Straight Stitch + Bullion Knot + Seed Beads

Cross-Stitch (twice) + Straight Stitch + Lazy Daisy

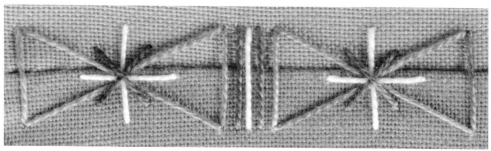

Cross-Stitch + Straight Stitch + Star Stitch

Detached Wheat Ear Stitch (2 colors)

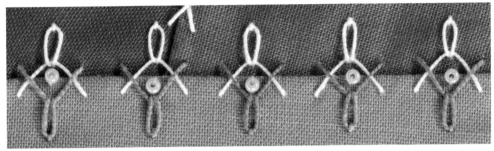

Detached Wheat Ear Stitch + Seed Beads

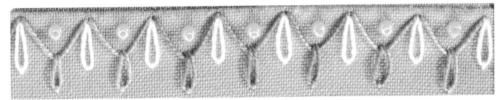

Detached Wheat Ear Stitch + Lazy Daisy + Seed Beads

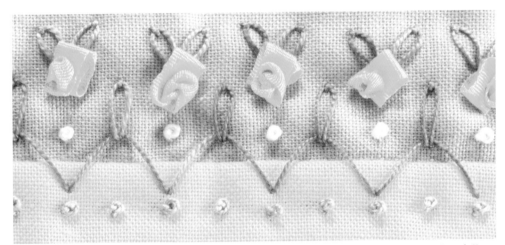

Detached Wheat Ear Stitch + Colonial Knot Running Stitch Rose (4mm silk ribbon) + Lazy Daisy + French Knot

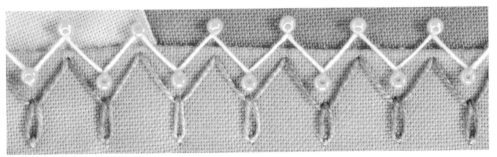

Detached Wheat Ear Stitch + Backstitch + Seed Beads

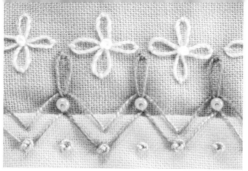

Detached Wheat Ear Stitch + Backstitch + Lazy Daisy + French Knot + Seed Beads

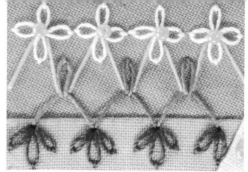

Detached Wheat Ear Stitch + Lazy Daisy + Straight Stitch + Seed Beads

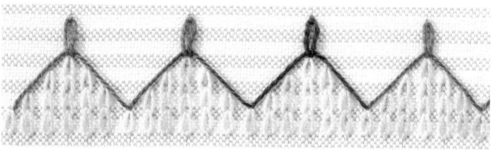

Detached Wheat Ear Stitch + Chain Stitch

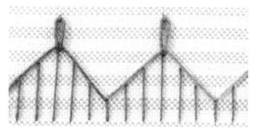

Detached Wheat Ear Stitch + Straight Stitch

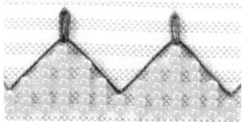

Detached Wheat Ear Stitch + Seed Beads

Detached Wheat Ear Stitch + Fly Stitch + Straight Stitch + Cross-Stitch + Backstitch + Pearls + Seed Beads

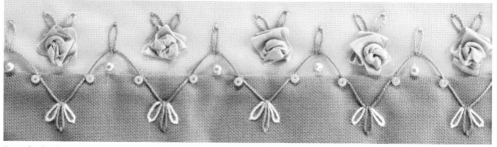

Detached Wheat Ear Stitch + Colonial Knot Running Stitch Rose (7mm silk ribbon) + Lazy Daisy + Pearls + Seed Beads

Featherstitch + Fly Stitch

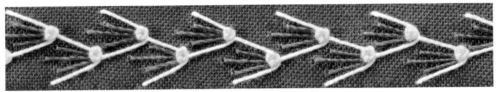

Featherstitch + Straight Stitch + French Knot

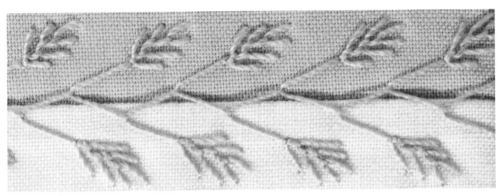

Featherstitch

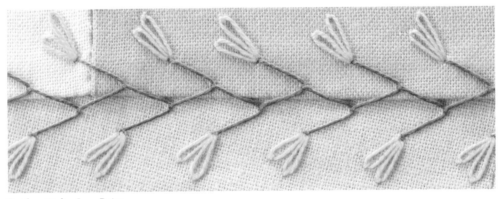

Featherstitch + Lazy Daisy

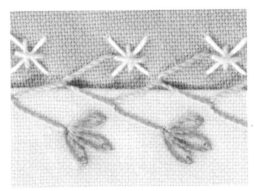

Featherstitch + Lazy Daisy + Star Stitch

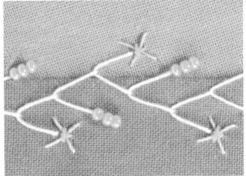

Featherstitch + Star Stitch + Seed Beads

Featherstitch + Lazy Daisy + Seed Beads

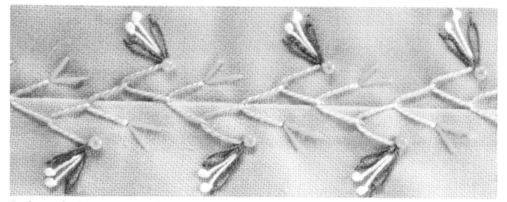

Featherstitch + Lazy Daisy + Pistil Stitch + Straight Stitch + Seed Beads

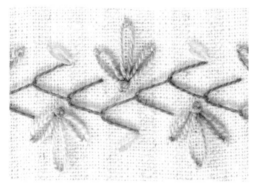

Featherstitch—Double + Lazy Daisy + French Knot

Featherstitch—Double + Lazy Daisy + French Knot

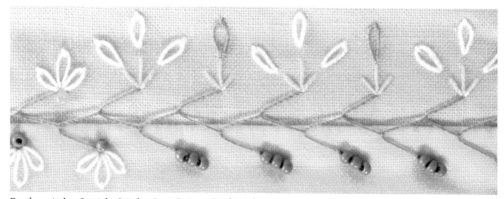

Featherstitch + Straight Stitch + Lazy Daisy + Seed Beads

Featherstitch + Straight Stitch + Lazy Daisy + Sequin Flower + Seed Bead

Featherstitch + Lazy Daisy + Fly Stitch + Straight Stitch

Featherstitch + Lazy Daisy + Straight Stitch + French Knot + Seed Beads

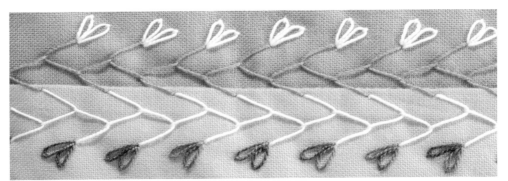

Featherstitch (twice) + Lazy Daisy

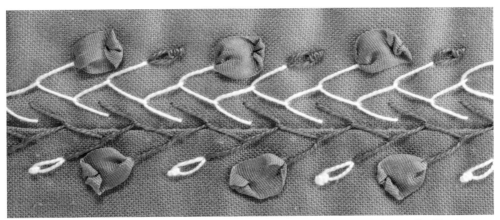

Featherstitch (twice) + Bullion Knot / Lazy Daisy Combination Stitch + Ribbon Stitch (7mm silk ribbon)

Featherstitch (twice) + Lazy Daisy + French Knot + Seed Beads

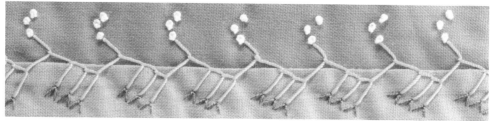

Featherstitch + French Knot + Straight Stitch

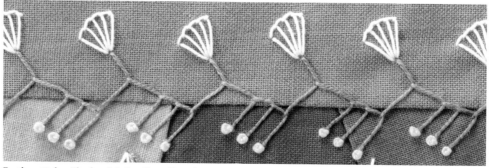

Featherstitch + Blanket Stitch—Fan + French Knot

Featherstitch + Star Stitch + French Knot

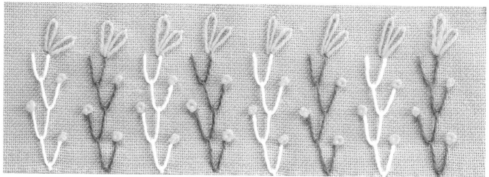

Featherstitch + Lazy Daisy + French Knot

Maidenhair Stitch Combinations

This stitch is often called the Maidenhair Stitch, but I decided to include it in the Featherstitch portion of this book. To make the stitch, follow the steps of the Featherstitch (page 114), but alter the placement of the individual stitches to match the photos of the Maidenhair Stitch.

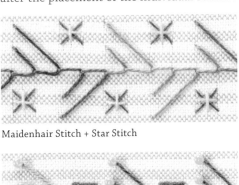

Maidenhair Stitch + Star Stitch

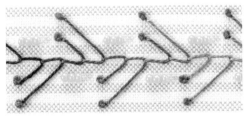

Maidenhair Stitch + French Knot + Seed Beads

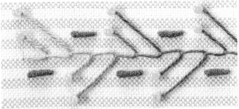

Maidenhair Stitch + Bullion Knot + Seed Beads

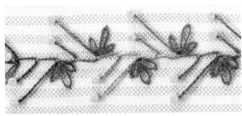

Maidenhair Stitch + Lazy Daisy + Seed Beads

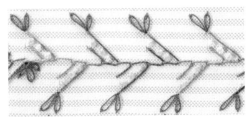

Maidenhair Stitch + Lazy Daisy + French Knot

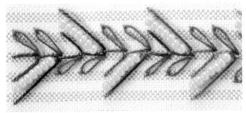

Maidenhair Stitch + Lazy Daisy + Seed Beads

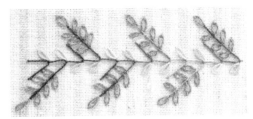

Maidenhair Stitch + Lazy Daisy

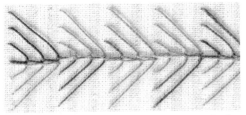

Maidenhair Stitch—Detached (alternating, 2 colors)

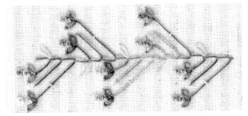

Maidenhair Stitch (Couched) + Lazy Daisy + French Knot

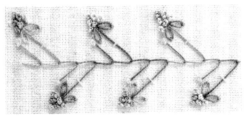

Maidenhair Stitch (Couched) + French Knot + Lazy Daisy + Straight Stitch

Fly Stitch + French Knot

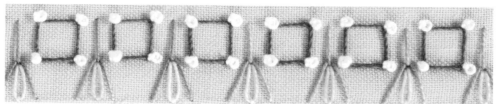

Fly Stitch + Lazy Daisy + Backstitch + French Knot

Fly Stitch + Lazy Daisy + Seed Beads

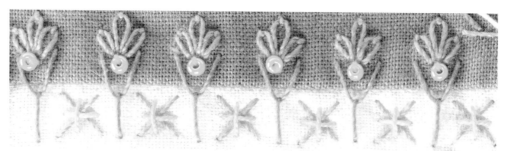

Fly Stitch + Lazy Daisy + Star Stitch + Seed Beads

Fly Stitch + Straight Stitch

Fly Stitch + Bullion Knots + Straight Stitch

Fly Stitch + Lazy Daisy

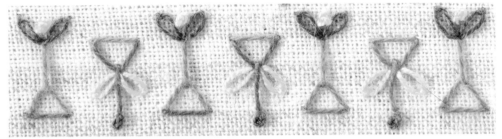

Fly Stitch + Lazy Daisy + Straight Stitch + French Knot

Fly Stitch + Lazy Daisy + French Knot

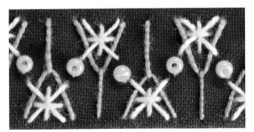

Fly Stitch + Star Stitch + Seed Beads

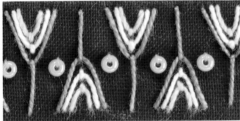

Fly Stitch + Seed Beads

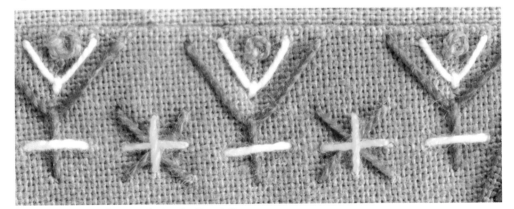

Fly Stitch + Star Stitch + Straight Stitch + French Knot

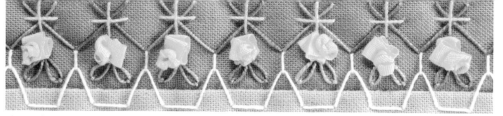

Fly Stitch + Straight Stitch + Herringbone Stitch—Detached + Cross-Stitch + Colonial Knot Running Stitch Rose (4mm silk ribbon) + Lazy Daisy

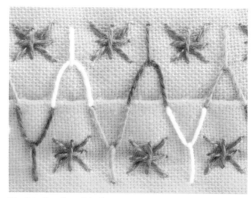

Fly Stitch + Star Stitch

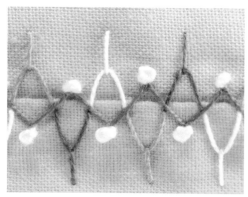

Fly Stitch + Backstitch + French Knot

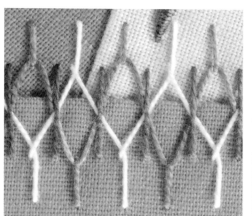

Fly Stitch + Cretan Stitch + Straight Stitch

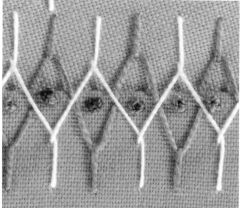

Fly Stitch + Cretan Stitch + French Knot

Fly Stitch + Straight Stitch + Cross-Stitch

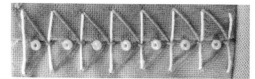

Fly Stitch + Straight Stitch (through tail of Fly Stitch) + Seed Beads

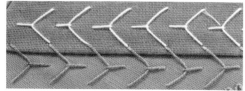

Fly Stitch

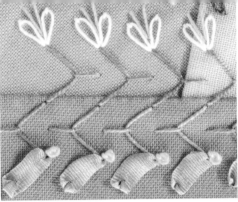

Fly Stitch + Ribbon Stitch (4mm silk ribbon) + French Knot + Lazy Daisy + Straight Stitch

Fly Stitch / Bullion Knot Combination + French Knot

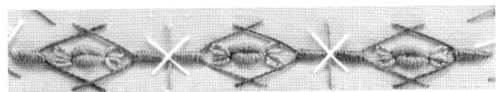

Fly Stitch / Bullion Knot Combination + Bullion Knot + Lazy Daisy + Straight Stitch + Cross-Stitch

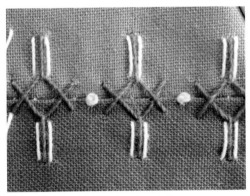

Fly Stitch + French Knot

Fly Stitch + Straight Stitch + French Knot

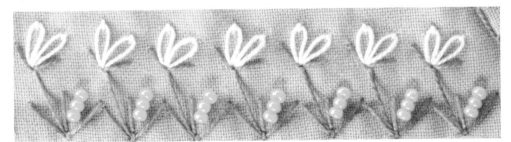

Fly Stitch (twice) + Straight Stitch + Lazy Daisy + Seed Beads

Fly Stitch + Lazy Daisy + French Knot + Seed Beads

Fly Stitch + Straight Stitch + French Knot

Herringbone Stitch + Straight Stitch

Herringbone Stitch + Straight Stitch + French Knot

Herringbone Stitch + Straight Stitch + Cross-Stitch

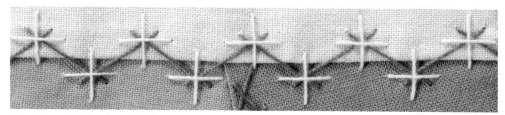

Herringbone Stitch + Cross-Stitch

Herringbone Stitch + Cross-Stitch + Stem Stitch (twice)

Herringbone Stitch + Cross-Stitch + Stem Stitch—Beaded

Herringbone Stitch + Cross-Stitch + Straight Stitch + Seed Beads

Herringbone Stitch + Straight Stitch + Star Stitch

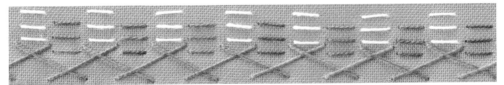

Herringbone Stitch + Straight Stitch

Herringbone Stitch + Straight Stitch

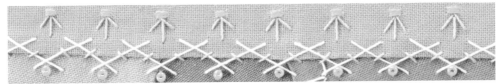

Herringbone Stitch + Straight Stitch + Seed Beads

Herringbone Stitch + Fly Stitch + French Knot

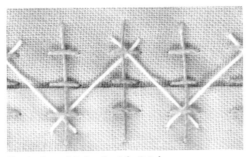

Herringbone Stitch + Straight Stitch

Herringbone Stitch + Cross-Stitch + Lazy Daisy

Herringbone Stitch + Straight Stitch + Lazy Daisy

Herringbone Stitch + Fly Stitch + Straight Stitch

Herringbone Stitch + Straight Stitch + Stem Stitch + Lazy Daisy

Herringbone Stitch (done 4 times)

Herringbone Stitch (twice, stacked with 2 colors of thread)

Herringbone Stitch (elongated on one side) + Straight Stitch

Herringbone Stitch + Lazy Daisy + Seed Beads

Herringbone Stitch + Lazy Daisy

Herringbone Stitch + Lazy Daisy

Herringbone Stitch + Straight Stitch + Bullion Knot + Lazy Daisy

Herringbone Stitch (twice) + Cross-Stitch

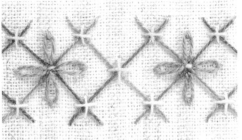

Herringbone Stitch (twice) + Cross-Stitch + Lazy Daisy + Straight Stitch

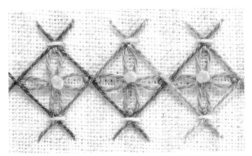

Herringbone Stitch (twice) + Straight Stitch + Lazy Daisy + French Knot

Herringbone Stitch (twice) + Cross-Stitch + Lazy Daisy + French Knot

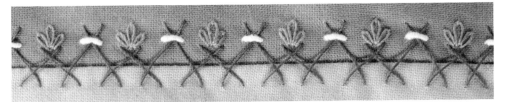

Herringbone Stitch (high-low) + Bullion Knot + Lazy Daisy

Herringbone Stitch—Detached + Straight Stitch

Herringbone Stitch—Detached + Cross-Stitch + Lazy Daisy + French Knot

Herringbone Stitch—Detached + Lazy Daisy + French Knot

Herringbone Stitch—Detached + Cross-Stitch + Straight Stitch

Herringbone Stitch—Detached + Straight Stitch + Star Stitch

Herringbone Stitch—Detached + Straight Stitch + Star Stitch

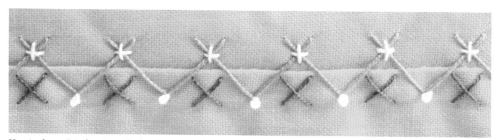

Herringbone Stitch—Detached + Cross-Stitch + French Knot

Herringbone Stitch—Detached + Straight Stitch + Backstitch

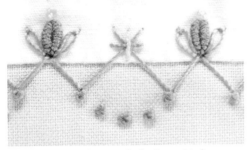

Herringbone Stitch—Detached + Cross-Stitch
(2 colors) + Bullion Knots + French Knot + Lazy Daisy

Herringbone Stitch—Detached + Cross-Stitch
(2 colors) + Bullion Knots + Lazy Daisy + Straight
Stitch + Seed Beads

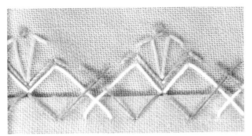

Herringbone Stitch—Detached (2 colors) +
Backstitch + French Knot

Herringbone Stitch—Detached (2 colors) +
Backstitch + Straight Stitch + Lazy Daisy + French
Knot + Seed Beads

Herringbone Stitch—Detached + Cross-Stitch

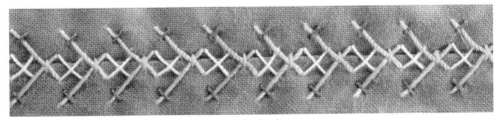

Herringbone Stitch—Detached + Cross-Stitch + Straight Stitch

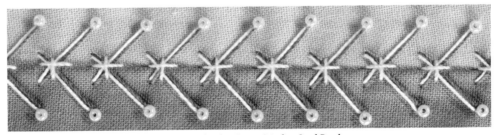

Herringbone Stitch—Detached (twice, in 2 colors) + Cross-Stitch + Seed Beads

Herringbone Stitch + Straight Stitch + Cross-Stitch + French Knot

Herringbone Stitch + Lazy Daisy + Cross-Stitch

Herringbone Stitch + Lazy Daisy + Cross-Stitch

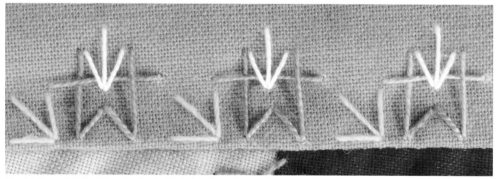

Herringbone Stitch—Detached + Backstitch + Straight Stitch

Herringbone Stitch—Detached + Straight Stitch + Sequin Flowers + French Knot

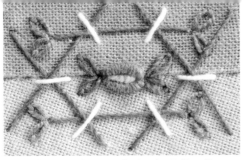

Herringbone Stitch + Straight Stitch + Bullion Rose +
Lazy Daisy

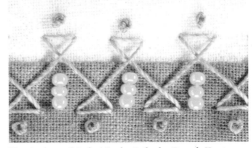

Herringbone Stitch—Backstitched + French Knot +
Seed Beads

Herringbone Stitch—Detached, Backstitched (2 colors) + Cross-Stitch

Herringbone Stitch—Detached, Backstitched + Herringbone Stitch—Detached + Cross-Stitch

Herringbone Stitch—Detached, Backstitched +
Straight Stitch + Lazy Daisy + Seed Beads

Herringbone Stitch—Detached, Backstitched +
Straight Stitch + Cross-Stitch + Bullion Roses + Lazy
Daisy

Herringbone Stitch—Backstitched + Blanket Stitch +
Backstitch + Cross-Stitch + Lazy Daisy + French Knot

Lazy Daisy + Sequin Flowers + French Knot

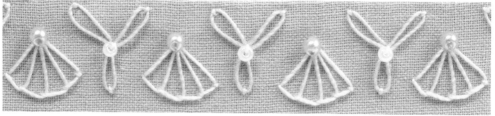

Lazy Daisy + Blanket Stitch—Fan + Seed Beads + Pearls

Lazy Daisy + Straight Stitch + French Knot

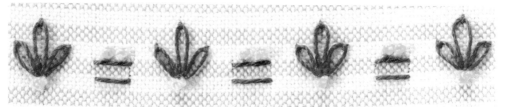

Lazy Daisy + Straight Stitch + French Knot

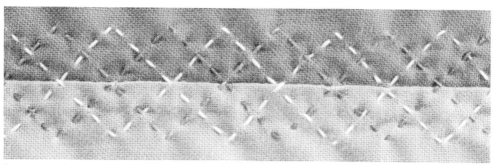

Running Stitch

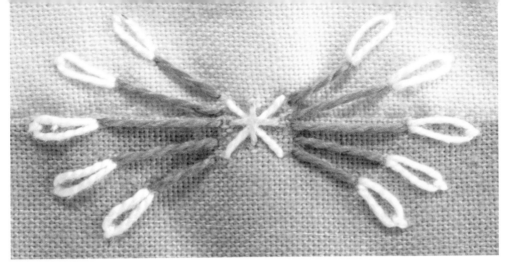

Star Stitch + Straight Stitch + Lazy Daisy

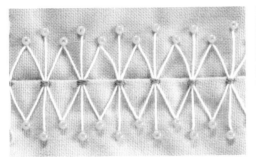

Sheaf Stitch + Seed Beads

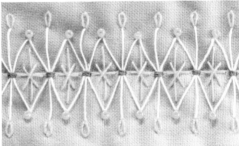

Sheaf Stitch + Star Stitch + Lazy Daisy + Seed Beads

Stem Stitch + Straight Stitch (Couched) + Ribbon Stitch (7mm silk ribbon)

Spider Web Rose (4mm silk ribbon) + Ribbon Stitch (7mm silk ribbon)

Colonial Knot Running Stitch Rose (for center) + Ribbon Stitch (7mm silk ribbon)

Colonial Knots (4mm silk ribbon) + Ribbon Stitch (7mm and 4mm silk ribbon) + Featherstitch Leaves

Ribbon Stitch (7mm silk ribbon) + Side Ribbon Stitch (7mm silk ribbon) + Straight Stitch (twisting the ribbon first with 4mm silk ribbon) + Ribbon Stitch (4mm silk ribbon). See Side Ribbon Stitch Flower (page 133) for the Side Ribbon Stitch.

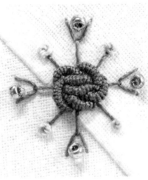

Bullion Rose + Fly Stitch + Straight Stitch + French Knot + Seed Beads

Fly Stitch + Lazy Daisy + Seed Beads + Rose Montée

Fly Stitch + French Knot + Seed Beads + Rose Montée

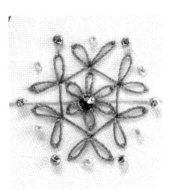

Backstitch + Lazy Daisy + French Knot + Seed Beads + Rose Montée

Fly Stitch + Lazy Daisy + French Knot + Star Stitch + Seed Beads + Rose Montée

Herringbone Stitch + Fly Stitch + French Knot + Seed Beads + Rose Montée

Fly Stitch + Detached Wheat Ear Stitch + Lazy Daisy + French Knot + Seed Beads + Rose Montée

Stem Stitch + Lazy Daisy + Seed Beads + Rose Montée

Spider Web Rose (stitched with thread) + Featherstitch leaves

Star Stitch + French Knot

Star Stitch + Lazy Daisy + French Knot

Star Stitch + Lazy Daisy + Seed Beads

Star Stitch + Colonial Knot Running Stitch Rose (7mm silk ribbon) + Lazy Daisy

Star Stitch + Lazy Daisy

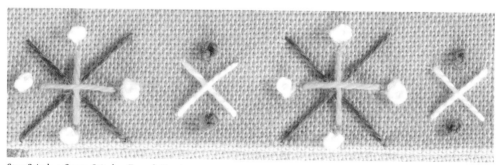

Star Stitch + Cross-Stitch + French Knot

Star Stitch + Straight Stitch

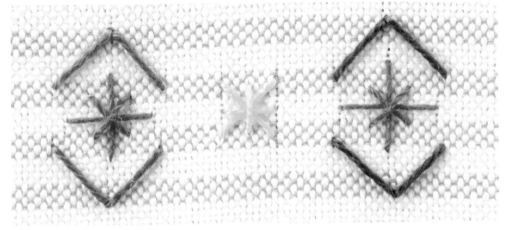

Star Stitch + Backstitch

Star Stitch + Straight Stitch + Fly Stitch + Seed Beads

Stem Stitch (3 colors)

Stem Stitch + Blanket Stitch

Stem Stitch + Featherstitch (2 colors)

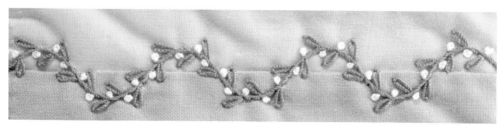

Stem Stitch + Lazy Daisy + French Knot

Stem Stitch + Lazy Daisy + Pistil Stitch

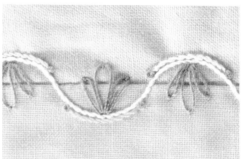

Stem Stitch (2 colors) + Lazy Daisy + French Knot

Stem Stitch + Lazy Daisy + Straight Stitch (Couched) + French Knot

Stem Stitch (2 colors) + Star Stitch + Lazy Daisy + French Knot

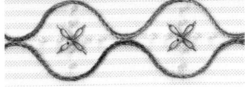

Stem Stitch (2 colors) + Lazy Daisy + French Knot + Seed Beads

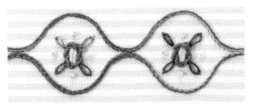

Stem Stitch (2 colors) + Bullion Rose + Lazy Daisy + French Knot

Stem Stitch + French Knot + Star Stitch + Fly Stitch + Straight Stitch

Stem Stitch + French Knot + Fly Stitch + Lazy Daisy

Stem Stitch + Star Stitch + Featherstitch

Stem Stitch + Star Stitch + Straight Stitch + Straight Stitch (Couched)

Stem Stitch (see pattern, page 73)

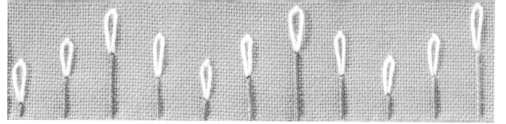

Straight Stitch + Lazy Daisy

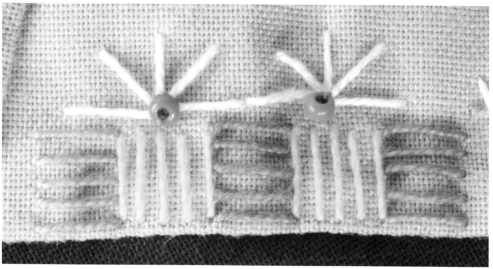

Straight Stitch + Seed Beads

Straight Stitch + Seed Beads

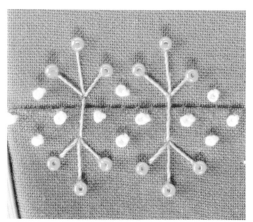

Straight Stitch + French Knot + Seed Beads

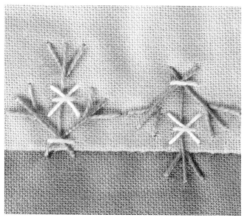

Straight Stitch + Cross-Stitch + Straight Stitch

Straight Stitch + Star Stitch

Straight Stitch + Lazy Daisy + Star Stitch + French Knot

Straight Stitch + Cross-Stitch (Couched) + Lazy Daisy

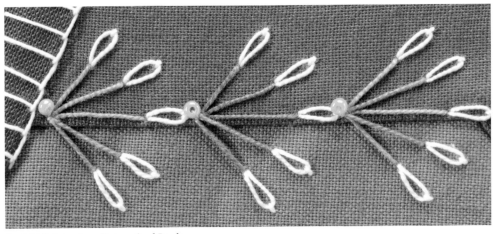

Straight Stitch + Lazy Daisy + Seed Beads

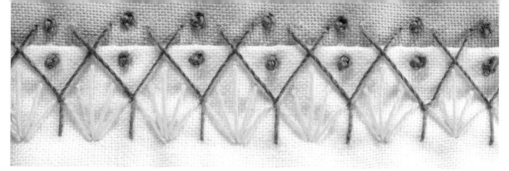

Cretan/Herringbone Combination Stitch + Straight Stitch + French Knot

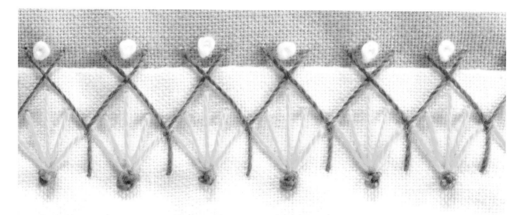

Cretan/Herringbone Combination Stitch + Straight Stitch + French Knot

Cretan/Herringbone Combination Stitch + Straight Stitch + Cross-Stitch + Sequin Flower + Seed Beads

Cretan/Herringbone Combination Stitch + Straight Stitch + Lazy Daisy + French Knot

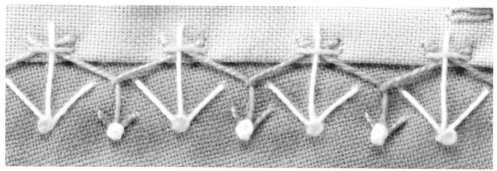

Cretan/Herringbone Combination Stitch + Straight Stitch + French Knot

Cretan/Herringbone Combination Stitch—Detached + Straight Stitch + Lazy Daisy + French Knot

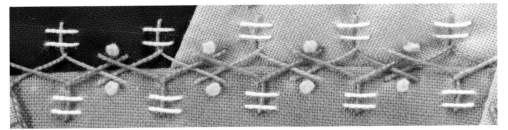

Cretan/Herringbone Combination Stitch (twice) + Straight Stitch + French Knot

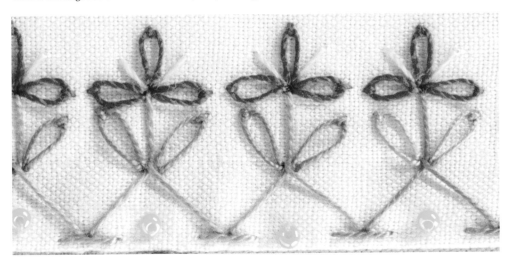

Chevron/Cretan Combination Stitch + Lazy Daisy + Straight Stitch + Seed Beads

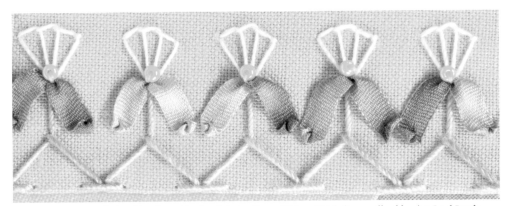

Chevron/Cretan Stitch Combination + Blanket Stitch—Fan + Ribbon Stitch (4mm silk ribbon) + Seed Beads

Daffodil Sampler

Crazy-Pieced Background in a Hoop

FINISHED SIZE: 5¼″ × 8¼″ (13.3 × 21cm) oval

This is a fun, small sampler that can be completed fairly quickly. I used a 5¼″ × 8¼″ (13.3 × 21cm) oval hoop to create this sampler, but you could use any size that you want.

Materials

MUSLIN: 7″ × 12″ (17.8 × 30.5cm) rectangle

ASSORTED SOLIDS: ⅛ yard (0.12m) of at least 5 different solid fabrics

ASSORTED THREADS: Variety of perle cotton #12 threads

PEARLS AND SEED BEADS

AIR-ERASABLE PEN (I used a purple Dritz Mark-B-Gone Marking Pen, Extra-Fine Point.)

GLUE (I used Aleene's Turbo Tacky Glue.)

COTTON SWAB

Making the Sampler

1. Use the air-erasable pen to trace the inside shape of the outer hoop onto the muslin. This gives you the size that you need to make your crazy-pieced sampler.

2. Referring to the Montano Centerpiece Method (page 139), piece the background. You don't need to piece the entire muslin rectangle, but make the crazy-pieced area at least 1″ (2.5cm) larger than the line you traced from the hoop.

3. Place the outer hoop on top of the pieced block and retrace the inside shape of the outer hoop. Stitch a large basting stitch on the line you just traced so you know where to place your stitches while embroidering.

4. Use the following stitch combinations (next page) to help you embroider your sampler, or you can try creating some of your own! Because the sampler is backed with muslin, I didn't use the hoop for support while embroidering.

Finishing

1. Place the finished block on top of the inside hoop and line it up with the basting stitches around the sampler. Place the outer hoop on top of the block and inner hoop. Gently pull on the outer edges of the block to tighten it up in the frame.

2. Turn the sampler wrong side up and trim the outer excess fabric to ½″ (1.2cm) from the hoop. Using a cotton swab, apply glue to the inside of the inner hoop. Fold the excess ½″ (1.2cm) of fabric to the inside hoop, and gently press so that it will stick to the hoop. Work your way around the hoop, placing clothespins as you go to keep the fabric in place. When the glue is dry, remove the clothespins and enjoy your project!

Tip When placing the clothespins on the hoop, make sure to place them where there are seams from crazy piecing to give that area extra support in adhering to the hoop.

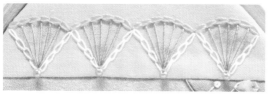

Chain Stitch + Straight Stitch + Pearls (page 24)

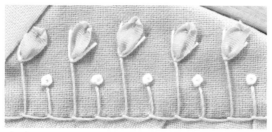

Blanket Stitch + Fly Stitch + French Knot + Ribbon Stitch (4mm silk ribbon) (page 15)

Chevron Stitch + Blanket Stitch—Fan + Seed Beads (page 26)

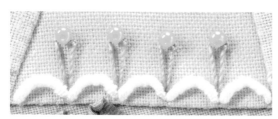

Bullion Knot + Straight Stitch + Seed Beads (page 22)

Backstitch + Fly Stitch + French Knot + Colonial Knot Running Stitch Rose (4mm silk ribbon) + Lazy Daisy (page 8)

Detached Blanket Stitch + Blanket Stitch—Fan + Seed Beads (page 16)

Chevron/Cretan Stitch Combination + Blanket Stitch—Fan + Ribbon Stitch (4mm silk ribbon) + Seed Beads (page 70)

Stem Stitch (see Regard pattern, below)

Lazy Daisy + Blanket Stitch—Fan + Seed Beads + Pearls (page 59)

-------------- Stitch Template --------------

Regard

Ribbon Stitch (7mm silk ribbon) + Side Ribbon Stitch (7mm silk ribbon) + Straight Stitch (twisting the ribbon first with 4mm silk ribbon) + Ribbon Stitch (4mm silk ribbon) (page 61)

Flowers and Vines Sampler

Solid Fabric Background in a Hoop

FINISHED SIZE:

9″ (22.9cm) diameter

Materials

BACKGROUND FABRIC: 12″ × 12″ (30.5 × 30.5cm) square

HOOP: 9″ (22.9cm) diameter

ASSORTED THREADS: Variety of perle cotton or silk twist #8 and #12 threads

SILK RIBBON: 4mm and 7mm

SEED BEADS

AIR-ERASABLE PEN (I used a purple Dritz Mark-B-Gone Marking Pen, Extra-Fine Point.)

GLUE (I used Aleene's Turbo Tacky Glue.)

COTTON SWAB

OPTIONAL: ⅞ yard (0.8m) of pompom fringe

Making the Sampler

1. Zigzag or whipstitch around the edges of the 12″ × 12″ (30.5 × 30.5cm) background square to prevent raveling while you are working.

2. To help with placement of the stitch combinations, use the air-erasable pen to draw concentric rings onto the background. Start by marking the inside edge of the outer hoop; then mark rings ½″, 1¾″, and 2⅞″ (1.2cm, 4.4cm, and 7.3cm) inside the first circle. Mark the center of the circles for placement of the center flower.

3. Place the background fabric in the hoop and make sure it is good and tight before you start your embroidery. I always use a hoop when working with a single piece of fabric like this but find I don't need a hoop when working on double thicknesses like the foundation-pieced backgrounds. The fabric will loosen as you stitch, but you can gently pull on the fabric edges to tighten it back up.

4. Start by stitching the stitch combination that is closest to the outer edge and work your way to the center of the hoop.

The stitch combinations at right are listed in the order that I stitched them, starting with the stitch combination closest to the outer edge. The descriptions below each photo are written in the order that I stitched the combinations.

5. When the embroidery is finished, make sure the outer layer of stitching is evenly placed from the hoop edge. You may gently pull on the outer edges of the fabric to move the sampler in place. Then trim and glue as described in Finishing (page 72). Add the optional pom-pom trim with glue.

Featherstitch + French Knot + Ribbon Stitch (7mm silk ribbon) + Seed Beads (page 31)

Featherstitch + Lazy Daisy (4mm silk ribbon and thread) + French Knot (page 31)

Featherstitch + Ribbon Stitch done on the left side of the ribbon (7mm silk ribbon) + Lazy Daisy (4mm silk ribbon and thread) + Seed Beads (page 31)

Spider Web Rose (4mm silk ribbon) + Ribbon Stitch (7mm silk ribbon) (page 60)

Pansy Sampler

Strip-Pieced Background

FINISHED SIZE: 5½″ × 12½″ (14 × 31.8cm)

Materials

MUSLIN: 5½″ × 12½″ (14 × 31.8cm)

ASSORTED SOLIDS: 4 fabrics, 2 strips 2″ × 5½″ (5.1 × 14cm) from each

SILK RIBBON: 4mm

FINE-POINT PERMANENT MARKER (I used a Sharpie.)

AIR-ERASABLE PEN (I used a purple Dritz Mark-B-Gone Marking Pen, Extra Fine Point.)

ASSORTED THREADS: Variety of perle cotton #12 threads

Making the Sampler

1. Following the guidelines in the Foundation-Piecing Tutorial (page 136), alternate and repeat the color strips as you sew them onto the muslin rectangle. Your sampler will be shorter than the one in the tutorial, but otherwise, all the instructions are the same.

2. Embroider each stitch combination onto the background, referring to the key for placement. The descriptions below each photo are written in the order that I stitched each combination.

3. Bind the sampler using the method of your choice.

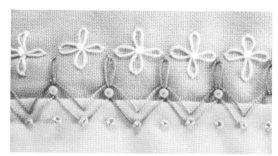

Detached Wheat Ear Stitch + Backstitch + Lazy Daisy +
French Knot + Seed Beads (page 41)

Detached Wheat Ear Stitch + Colonial Knot Running
Stitch Rose (4mm silk ribbon) + Lazy Daisy + French Knot
(page 40)

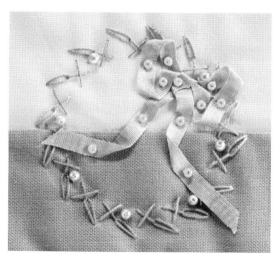

Chain Stitch—Feathered + Straight Stitch + Pearls + Silk
Ribbon Bow (4mm silk ribbon; Couched with Seed Beads)
(page 25)

Detached Wheat Ear Stitch + Fly Stitch + Straight Stitch +
Cross-Stitch + Backstitch + Pearls + Seed Beads (page 41)

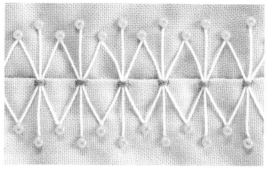

Sheaf Stitch + Seed Beads (page 60)

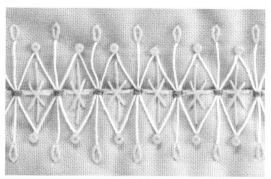

Sheaf Stitch + Star Stitch + Lazy Daisy + Seed Beads
(page 60)

Chain Stitch—Feathered + French Knot (page 25)

Detached Wheat Ear Stitch + Colonial Knot Running Stitch
Rose (7mm silk ribbon) + Lazy Daisy + Pearls + Seed Beads
(page 41)

Fly Stitch + Straight Stitch + Herringbone Stitch—
Detached + Cross-Stitch + Colonial Knot Running Stitch
Rose (4mm silk ribbon) + Lazy Daisy (page 49)

Hoop Holder

Crazy-Pieced Background

FINISHED SIZE: 13″ × 23½″ (33 × 59.7cm) open, 13″ × 11½″ (33 × 29.8cm) closed

Materials

MUSLIN: ½ yard (0.5m)

ASSORTED SOLIDS: 5 fat quarters for pieced outside

LINING SOLID: ¾ yard (0.7m) for lining, binding, and button loop

POCKET FABRIC:

> **COORDINATING PREQUILTED FABRIC:** ⅜ yard (0.34m) for pocket
>
> *or*
>
> **COORDINATING PRINT AND COTTON BATTING:** ⅜ yard (0.34m) *each* for pocket

FUSIBLE BATTING: ¾ yard (0.7m)

LIGHTWEIGHT KNIT INTERFACING, 20″ (46CM) WIDE: ½ yard (0.5m) (I used Pellon EK130 Easy-Knit fusible interfacing.)

1″ (2.5CM) BUTTON

ASSORTED THREADS: Variety of perle cotton #12 threads

AIR-ERASABLE PEN (I used a purple Dritz Mark-B-Gone Marking Pen, Extra Fine Point.)

OPTIONAL: Guitar purse strap

Cutting

MUSLIN

- Cut 1 rectangle 13 × 23½″ (33 × 59.7cm).

LINING SOLID

- Cut 1 rectangle 13 × 23½″ (33 × 59.7cm) for the lining.

- Cut 3 strips 2½″ (6.4cm) × width of fabric for the binding.

- Cut 1 rectangle 1½″ × 6½″ (3.8 × 16.5cm) for the button loop.

- *Optional:* Cut 2 rectangles 1½″ × 2¼″ (3.8 × 5.7cm) for the optional strap loops.

POCKET FABRIC

Coordinating prequilted fabric
- Cut 1 rectangle 13″ × 14″ (33 × 35.6cm).

Coordinating print
- Cut 2 rectangles 13″ × 14″ (33 × 35.6cm).

Cotton batting
- Cut 1 rectangle 13″ × 14″ (33 × 35.6cm).

FUSIBLE BATTING

- Cut 1 rectangle 13″ × 23½″ (33 × 59.7cm).

LIGHTWEIGHT KNIT INTERFACING

- Cut 1 rectangle 13″ × 23½″ (33 × 59.7cm) for the lining.

Making the Hoop Holder

Piecing the Background

1. Place the muslin rectangle on top of the curved corner shape (page 82). Align the straight edges of the corner with the straight edges of the curved corner shape, and mark the curve on the muslin with a fine-tip permanent marker. Repeat this for each of the 4 corners of the muslin. Cut the curve of each of the 4 corners of the muslin rectangle.

2. Use the trimmed muslin rectangle as a pattern to trim the corners of the lining, interfacing, and fusible batting rectangles. Set the lining, interfacing, and batting pieces aside.

3. Begin piecing the hoop holder, referring to Crazy Quilt Piecing (page 139). This is a fairly large area to piece, so I would recommend using the Montano Centerpiece instructions. When piecing, visualize how you would like the crazy quilting to look on each side when the hoop holder is closed. I started in the centers of both "sides" of the hoop holder. Keep working your way out until you meet in the middle of the hoop holder. To finish, you will need to hand appliqué the final few pieces into place.

4. Once the piecing is done, sew around the perimeter of the block ⅛″ (3mm) from the edge to keep the outer edges of the fabric in place. It works best if you sew around the perimeter muslin side up.

Embellishing

Embellish your hoop holder to your heart's content! Use a good variety of threads that will show up well on the fabrics that you have chosen. You may refer to the stitch combination section (page 7) for inspiration.

Assembling and Finishing

1. Press the interfacing to the wrong side of the hoop holder block, following the manufacturer's instructions. This step will help stabilize the block and keep the embroidery thread from coming loose.

2. To make the pocket section on the inside of the hoop holder, the instructions will vary depending on whether you purchased prequilted fabric.

For prequilted fabric, bind the 2 edges that measure 13″ (33cm) with your favorite binding method.

For fabric that needs to be quilted, layer the pieces as follows, bottom to top:

- One rectangle of pocket fabric, wrong side up

- The rectangle of cotton batting

- The other rectangle of pocket fabric, right side up

Pin the layers together. Following the diagram below, quilt the fabric every 2″ (5.1cm). I used a walking foot to do this quilting, but it isn't necessary. After you have quilted the layers, bind the 2 edges that measure 13″ (33cm) using your favorite binding method.

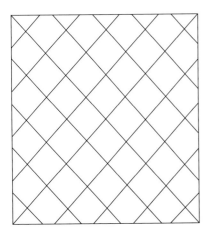

3. Place the embellished piece wrong side up, add the cotton batting, and finally add the lining fabric, right side up. Pin in place and baste around the outer edge.

4. Center the quilted pocket section on top of the lining of the hoop holder, matching the raw edges. Baste the raw edges through all the layers to keep the pocket in place.

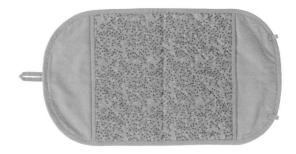

5. Sew down the center of the pocket through all the layers. This will keep your pocket in place.

6. To make the button loop, fold the 1½″ × 6½″ (3.8 × 16.5cm) rectangle of lining fabric in half lengthwise and press. Open the piece and fold the 2 raw edges toward the fold; press again. Fold the piece in half lengthwise again and sew the outer 2 folds together.

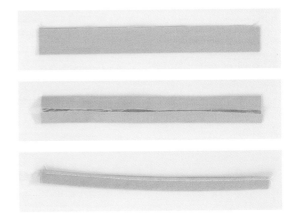

7. Fold the button loop and sew as pictured below.

8. Decide which side of your hoop holder will be the front and which will be the back. Pin the button loop as pictured to the top of the back of the hoop holder and baste into place.

9. Bind the hoop holder around the entire raw edge using your preferred method of choice.

10. Sew a 1″ (2.5cm) button on the front of the hoop holder approximately 1½″ (3.8cm) from the bound edge, making sure it is centered.

As an option, I decided to add a guitar purse strap to my hoop holder so I could wear it just like I would a cross-body purse. Amazon has a beautiful array of guitar purse straps to choose from! The guitar purse strap has a clip on each end, so it was very simple to make it a part of the hoop holder. You will need to make loops you can attach the clips to that are a part of your hoop holder.

OPTIONAL:
Loop Attachments for Strap

1. Follow the instructions for the button loop in Assembly and Finishing, Step 6 (previous page) to make 2 loops with the small rectangles.

2. For each loop, sew the raw edges together and turn them to the inside of your loop.

3. Sew the loops through all thickness just below the binding on the inside of the front side of the hoop holder. They will work best if placed about 4″ (10.2cm) from the center front and extending at least ½″ (1.2cm) from the top edge of the binding.

4. Clip the guitar strap to the loops, and you are ready to go!

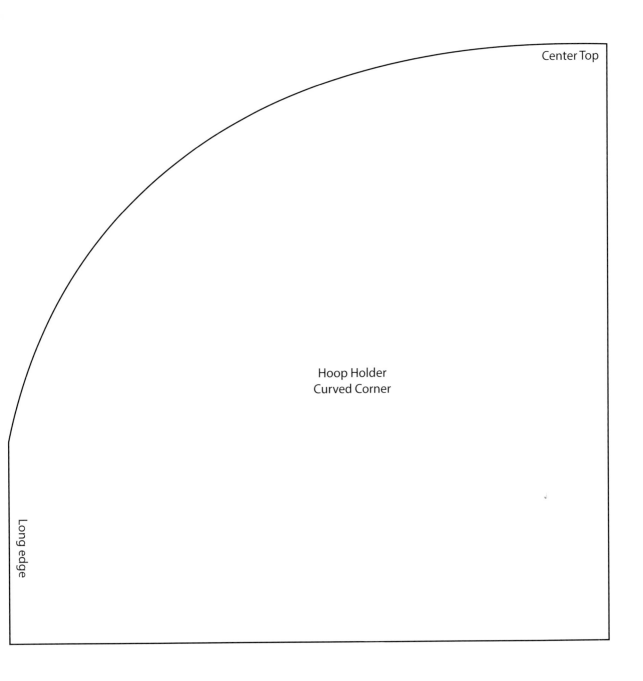

Center Top

Hoop Holder
Curved Corner

Long edge

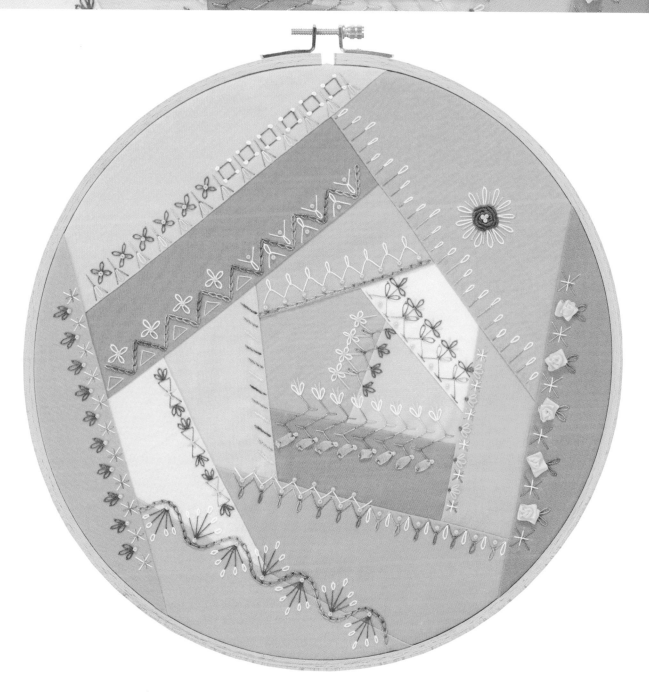

Pink is my favorite color, so I loved every minute of making this sampler.

I made this rainbow sampler because I loved making the first one (page 136). I thought about making a whole quilt like this but changed my mind after this one was done!

Here's another rainbow sampler using pastel colors instead. I incorporated my love for pink into the mix.

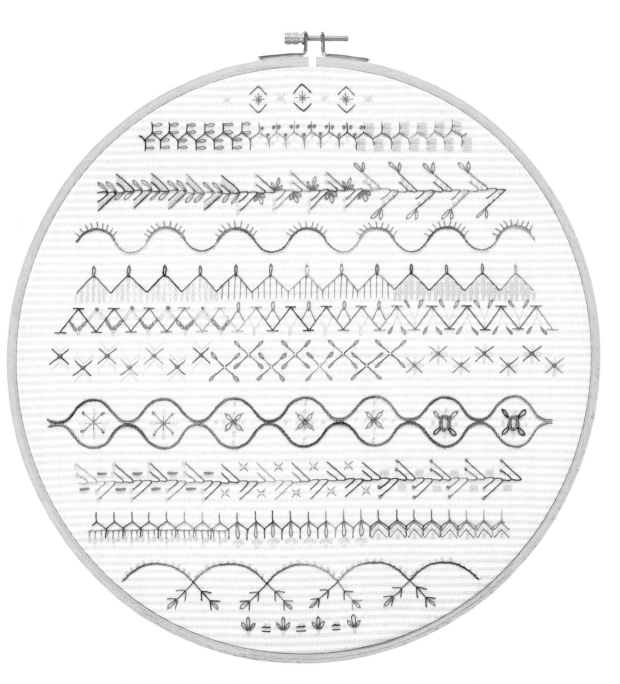

A men's striped shirt from a thrift store looks great, and you can also use the stripes to help make your stitches even.

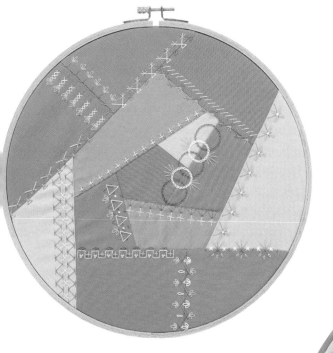

I have a whole rainbow of solid-color fabrics in my stash, so I felt drawn to putting these fabrics together. The bright pinks show up well in contrast to the fabrics.

I used purple fabrics for the blocks in the quilt that was featured in my last book, and I still had some scraps! I loved the pop of pinks used in this sampler as well as the yellow beading. I painted the hoop a bright pink with acrylic paints to help the stitches stand out even more.

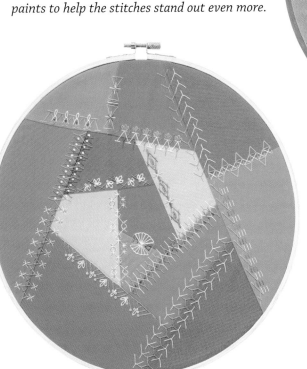

As with the purple hoop, these green colors were also very prevalent in my last book. It seems I always have to work pink into every project!

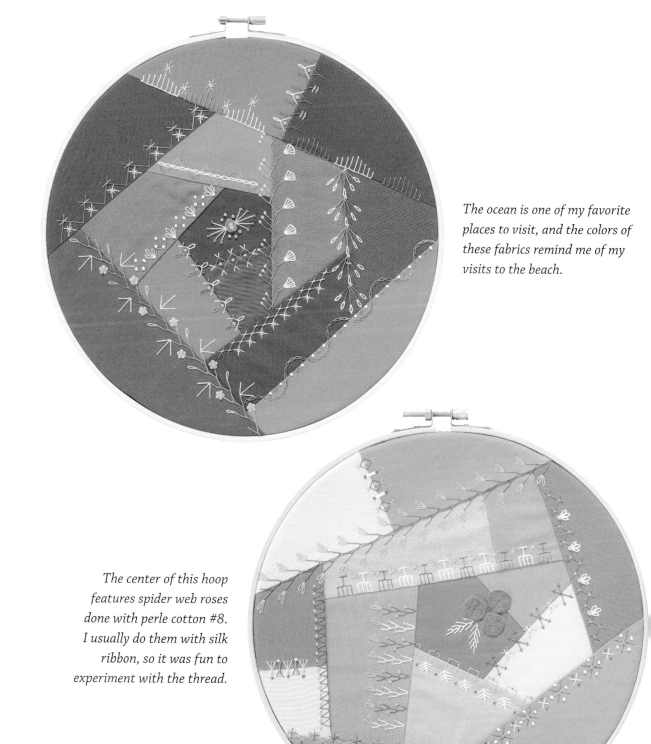

The ocean is one of my favorite places to visit, and the colors of these fabrics remind me of my visits to the beach.

The center of this hoop features spider web roses done with perle cotton #8. I usually do them with silk ribbon, so it was fun to experiment with the thread.

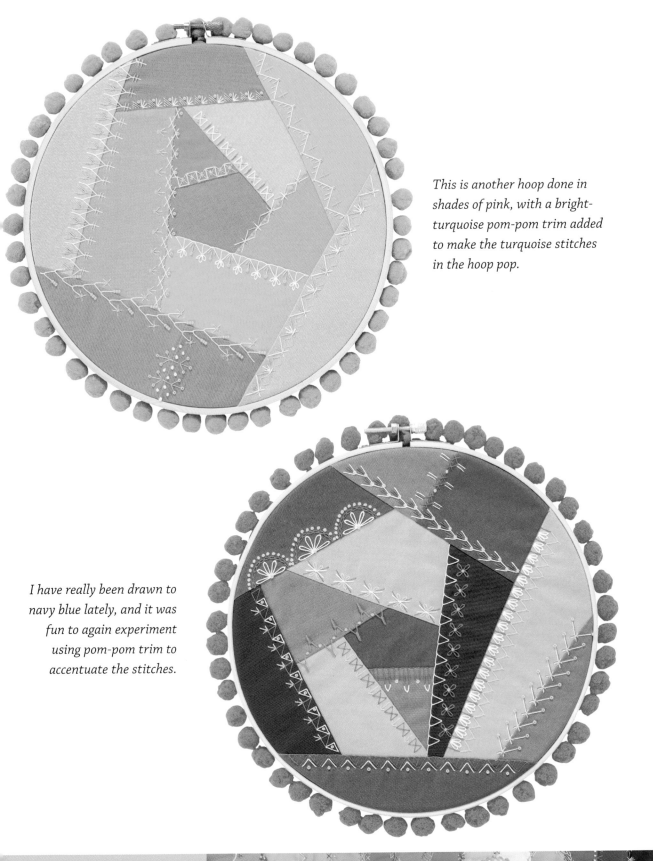

This is another hoop done in shades of pink, with a bright-turquoise pom-pom trim added to make the turquoise stitches in the hoop pop.

I have really been drawn to navy blue lately, and it was fun to again experiment using pom-pom trim to accentuate the stitches.

I decided to try making a sampler out of a traditional quilt block. A simple Nine-Patch block was fun, and the seams are really short, making it a quick project!

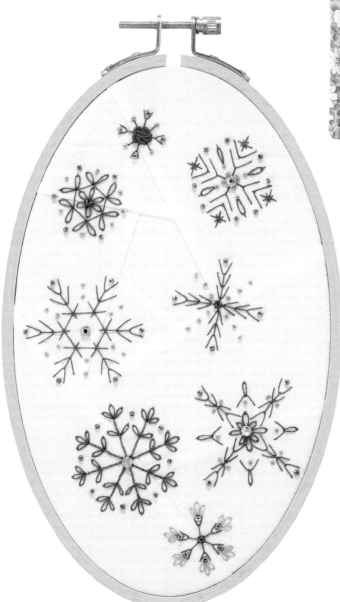

This snowflake sampler was a fun way to challenge myself to come up with different ways to embroider them.

Hand Embroidery Tools and Techniques

Hand-Stitching Tools

My love for hand stitching began at the age of eleven, when I found a red Christmas tin in the linen closet that was filled with embroidery floss. I started with simple projects such as tea towels and moved up to embroidering denim shirts, which was all the rage in those days. Hand embroidery is relaxing, and easy to take with you and work on wherever you go. The supplies are basic: threads, needles, scissors, and fabric or a crazy quilt block to work on. It always feels good to create something that is one of a kind. I tend to do most of my embroidering on crazy quilts, but it can also be used to dress up just about anything.

Needles

When choosing a needle for hand embroidery, there are four things I think about: the thread size, the type of project, the fabric the project is made of, and the type of embroidery stitches. For projects that are a single layer of fabric, such as an embroidery design done on muslin, an embroidery needle is the best choice. It is narrow and has a sharp point, and the shaft is elongated.

For crazy quilt embroidery, a chenille needle is what I reach for. It is wider, has a bigger eye, and has a sharp point to go through multiple layers of fabric. It is also the best choice if you are using a heavier thread, metallic thread, or silk ribbon. My favorite size chenille needle sizes are #22 and #24.

For bullion embroidery, a milliners needle is the best choice. It has an elongated shaft, which gives you room to wrap the thread around the needle, and a smaller eye to make pulling the thread off of the needle easier.

Needles come in different sizes—the smaller the number, the larger the eye of the needle. The thread size determines which size needle you should use. The thread should slide easily through the eye of the needle. You may need a larger needle size if you are having problems pulling the thread through the fabric. The eye of a needle is made to thread from one side, so if you are having trouble threading a needle, turn it to the other side.

Thread and Fabric Choices

When making thread choices, I think about the types of fabrics I am using. If it is a wool project, I use a heavier thread such as perle cotton #5 or #8, but if I am working on silk, I use a finer thread such as a perle cotton #12 or a silk twist. There are many beautiful threads to choose from, but my favorites tend to be hand-dyed cottons or silks.

For all the projects in this book, I used a variety of fabrics to change the look of the sampler. Some of the samplers used Kona Cotton solid fabrics (by Robert Kaufman Fabrics). Some of the other samplers used fabrics such as a men's striped shirt from the thrift store or a piece of striped linen. Don't be afraid to experiment with different fabrics to change the look of your project! Because I like my stitching to be the star of the project, I tend to use solid fabrics a lot so that there is nothing distracting the eye from seeing the embroidery. The best advice I can give you for thread and fabric choices is to use what you love! Then you will love what you are doing.

Tip When you are embroidering, the tension on the thread is very important! If you pull the thread too hard, the fabric will pucker, and if you leave it too loose, the stitches won't have a crisp look.

Hoop

When I work on a project that is a single layer of fabric, such as an embroidery design on a cotton fabric, I use a Q-Snap frame. Pick a size that fits comfortably in your hands. If a hoop is too large, it can be difficult to reach to the center. For larger projects, use a smaller hoop and move it around on the project. When you are done embroidering for a while, it is a good idea to remove the hoop to avoid getting permanent creases in the project.

When I work on a project that is a single layer of fabric, such as some of the wholecloth sampler hoops in this book, I use the hoop that will eventually become the frame to the project. For the samplers in this book that consist of a crazy quilt block, I don't use a hoop because I feel that the thickness of the fabrics gives the project enough stability for embroidery.

Even Stitch Tips

I love to make my stitches as even as possible—it's just the way I am! Over the years, I have found a few things that make my life simpler by helping me stitch more quickly without agonizing over every single stitch.

Tiger Tape

One of my favorite secret weapons is Tiger Tape. This is a tape that quilters use to make their stitches even when they are hand quilting. Tiger Tape comes in different widths and stitch sizes.

Chevron stitch using Tiger Tape. Notice that not only can you make the diagonal line even by counting over 4 dashes but you can also make the bar on the top consistently the same size.

Herringbone stitch using Tiger Tape

Blanket stitch using Tiger Tape

One word of caution: Tiger Tape should not be used on velvets. Pulling off the tape pulls out the tufts of velvet. Trust me, I know from personal experience!

Stitch Templates

These stitching templates have made my embroidery so much easier! I use a purple air-erasable pen (Dritz Mark-B-Gone Marking Pen, Extra-Fine Point) most of the time, but for dark fabrics I use a chalk pencil by either Sewline or Bohin. At right are a few ideas of how they can be used to achieve perfect stitches every time! You can purchase these templates from me in my Etsy shop, ThePinkBunny. For more instructions on how to use these templates, visit my website: valeriebothell.com.

Note: For demonstration purposes, I used a water-erasable pen in the images. I never use them on a regular basis—many of the fabrics I work with would not look good after getting wet!

Lay the template on the fabric and mark the dots with an air-erasable pen. Stitch your chosen embroidery stitch as usual, using the dots as a guide.

Chevron stitch using crazy quilt grid templates

Herringbone stitch using crazy quilt grid templates

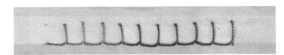

Blanket stitch using crazy quilt grid templates

Embroidery Stitch Reference

I love everything about crazy quilting, but hands down, my favorite part is the hand embroidery! For me, it is the great reward after doing all the piecing, and it really begins to "dress up" a crazy quilt block. What might look like a plain, ordinary block can turn into a real treasure when you spend a little time doing some handwork.

Striped fabric is a great choice for background fabric. Stripes always draw attention, and the straight lines can guide your stitch placement. All the stitches in this section are demonstrated on striped fabric; you may do this as you practice, or you can start on a crazy quilt seam.

When working on the stitches, I encourage you to try combining the stitches in different ways. You can use different stitches to create a seam with dimension by building the seam up one stitch at a time.

Starting with a basic featherstitch, add lazy daisy stitches, ribbon stitches, and pearls to create more interest to the stitch.

Crazy Quilt Stitches

Backstitch

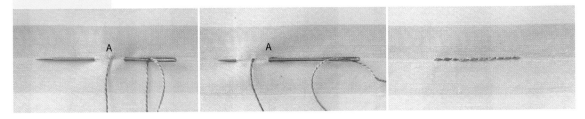

1. Bring up the needle on the edge of the stripe or crazy quilt seam at A. Take a stitch to the left, as shown.

2. Pull the needle to the front of the fabric. Move the needle to the right and take a stitch back to A, using the same hole that was made in Step 1. In the same movement, take a stitch to the left, as shown.

3. Continue as needed.

Tip ⁓ The backstitch is very versatile, and I use it for many different applications. When I use it to outline an object or a monogram, I make my stitches smaller than when I use it as a base in combination stitches.

Blanket Stitch

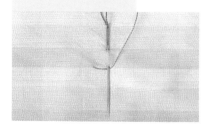

1. Bring up the needle on the lower edge of the stripe or crazy quilt seam. Move the needle to the right, placing it in a perpendicular position. Make sure the thread is *under* the needle, as shown.

Tip You can change the look of all of the different blanket stitch forms by varying the width, height, and angle of the stitch. Experiment and see what different looks you can come up with.

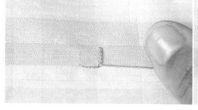

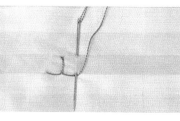

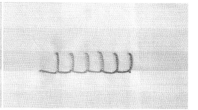

2. Pull the needle out of the fabric, and gently pull the thread to the right. Hold it in place with your left thumb.

3. Move the needle to the right, and take a stitch in the same manner as you did before.

4. Continue as needed.

Blanket Stitch—Beaded 1

For this stitch, use a needle with an eye big enough for the thread but small enough to go through the hole of the bead. An embroidery needle usually works well for this purpose.

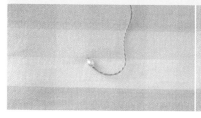

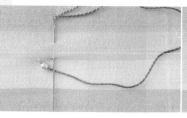

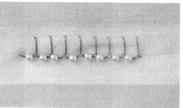

1. Bring up the needle on the lower edge of the stripe or crazy quilt seam, and string a bead on the thread.

2. Move the needle to the right, placing it in a perpendicular position. Make sure the thread is *under* the needle and the bead is to the left of the needle.

3. Continue as needed.

Blanket Stitch—Beaded 2

For demonstration purposes, I used red beading thread to make it easier to see the stitch. Normally, I use a thread that matches either the fabric or the bead, depending on the project.

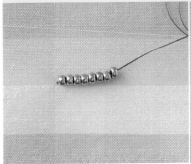

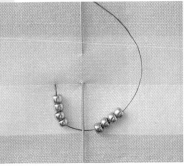

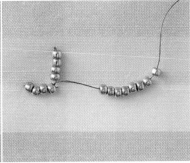

1. Bring up the needle on the lower edge of the stripe or crazy quilt seam, and string 8 beads on the thread.

2. Move the needle to the right, placing it in a perpendicular position. Make sure the thread is *under* the needle and that there are 4 beads to the left of the needle and 4 to the right.

3. Pull the needle to the front of the fabric, and string 8 more beads on the thread. Repeat Step 2.

4. Continue as needed, taking the needle to the back of the fabric just on the other side of the thread that formed the last loop.

Blanket Stitch—Circular

For demonstration purposes, I used a pen to mark my circle. Normally, I use a purple air-erasable pen that fades away after I finish stitching.

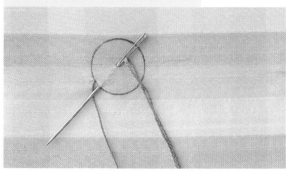 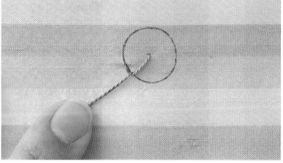

1. Draw a circle on the fabric and mark the center. Bring up the needle on the outer edge of the circle, and take a stitch from the center mark, moving the needle under the fabric to the outer edge of the circle. Make sure the thread is *under* the needle.

2. Pull the thread away from the circle until the stitch lies flat on the fabric. Keep consistent tension on the thread. If you pull the thread too hard, the fabric will pucker, and if you leave it too loose, the stitches won't have a crisp look.

3. Continue around the circle, using the same hole in the center for each stitch until there is 1 last stitch to complete it. Place the needle under the thread from the first stitch; then take the needle to the back of the fabric in the center hole. *Make sure not to pull too tightly, or you will distort the circle.*

Blanket Stitch—Closed

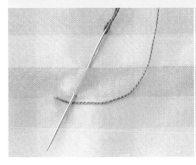
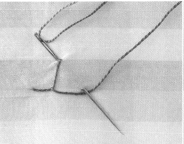
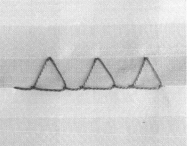

1. Bring up the needle on the lower edge of the stripe or crazy quilt seam. Take a stitch to the right, placing it at an angle. Make sure the thread is *under* the needle, as shown.

2. Pull the needle out of the fabric, and gently pull the thread to the right. Hold it in place with your left thumb, as shown in Blanket Stitch, Step 2 (page 95). Take a stitch to the right, placing it at an angle to make the 2 stitches come to a point. Take a stitch in the same manner as before.

3. Continue as needed.

Blanket Stitch—Crossed

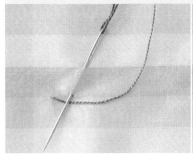
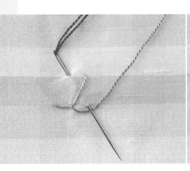
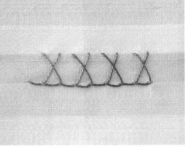

1. Bring up the needle on the lower edge of the stripe or a crazy quilt seam. Move the needle to the right, placing it at an angle. Make sure the thread is *under* the needle, as shown.

2. Pull the needle out of the fabric, and gently pull the thread to the right. Hold it in place with your left thumb, as shown in Blanket Stitch, Step 2 (page 95). Take a stitch to the right, placing it at an angle to make the 2 stitches cross. Take a stitch in the same manner as before.

3. Continue as needed.

Blanket Stitch—Fan

For demonstration purposes, I used a pen to mark my fan shape. Normally, I use a purple air-erasable pen that fades away after I finish stitching.

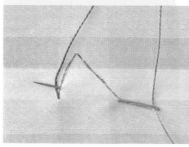  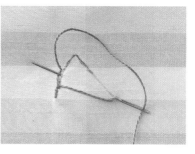

1. Draw a fan shape on the fabric. Bring up the needle on the fan's lower outer edge, and take a stitch from the end of the fan's slanted line, moving the needle under the fabric to the fan's outer edge. Make sure the thread is *under* the needle.

2. Pull the thread away from the fan until the stitch lies flat on the fabric. Keep consistent tension on the thread. If you pull the thread too hard, the fabric will pucker, and if you leave it too loose, the stitches won't have a crisp look.

3. Continue stitching the fan shape. When taking the stitch at the end of the fan's slanted line, get as close to the first stitch as possible without crossing the threads.

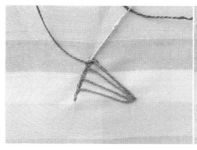 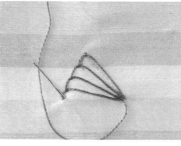

4. When the fan shape is completed, take the needle to the back of the fabric just on the other side of the thread that formed the last blanket stitch.

5. To complete the lower edge of the fan shape, bring up the needle up just below the first stitch done at the end of the slanted line. Take the needle to the back of the fabric where the first stitch was started on the lower edge of the fan shape.

Blanket Stitch—Knotted

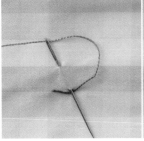  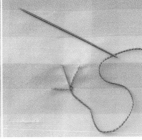 

1. Bring up the needle on the lower edge of the stripe or a crazy quilt seam. Take a stitch to the right, placing it at an angle. Make sure the thread is *under* the needle, as shown.

2. Take a stitch that starts at the base of the blanket stitch and angles to the right. Loop the thread around the needle and make sure the thread is *under* the needle, as shown.

3. Pull the needle and thread toward you until the stitch lies flat on the fabric.

4. Continue as needed.

Blanket/Cretan Combination Stitch

Refer to Blanket Stitch (page 95) and Cretan Stitch (page 110) as needed.

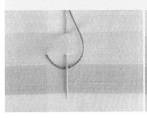 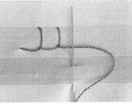 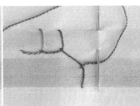 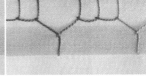

1. Bring up the needle on the lower edge of the stripe or a crazy quilt seam. Move the needle to the right, placing it in a perpendicular position with the needle going in a downward direction as you take the stitch. Make sure the thread is *under* the needle.

2. Repeat Step 1 to make another blanket stitch. Move the needle to the right, and place the needle in a perpendicular position on the opposite side of the striped fabric or the seam, making sure the needle is moving in an upward direction as you take the stitch.

3. Move the needle to the right. Repeat Steps 1 and 2 as needed.

Blanket/Herringbone Combination Stitch

See Herringbone/Blanket Combination Stitch (page 121).

Bullion Knot

For this stitch, use a milliners needle in a size 3 or 5, depending on the size of the thread.

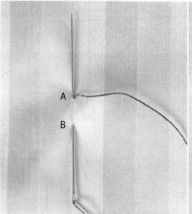
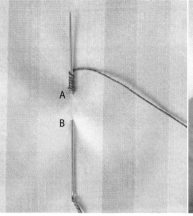
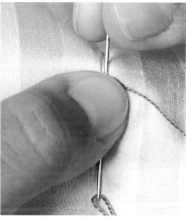

1. Pull the needle and thread to the front of the fabric at A. Take a stitch about ¼˝ (6mm) to B, and push the tip of the needle to come out at A again, but make sure not to pull the needle through the fabric. Hold the base of the needle and fabric in your left hand, pushing the tip of the needle up and away from the fabric. Pick up the thread coming out at A with your right hand.

2. Wrap the thread around the tip of the needle in a clockwise direction. The wraps around the needle need to be at least equal to the space between A and B.

3. When you have enough wraps on the needle, cover and hold the wraps with your left thumb. Pull the needle through the wraps with your right hand, pulling the thread in an upward motion until the bullion wraps are nearly down to the fabric.

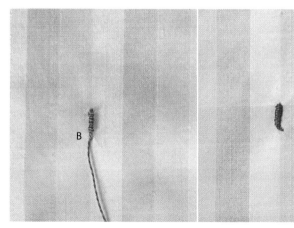

4. Pull the needle and thread toward B, laying the wraps flat against the fabric until there is no slack in the thread. Straighten any wraps that need straightening by rubbing your finger over them until they lie smooth. Push the needle and thread to the back of the fabric at B.

Bullion Knot/Fly Stitch Combination Stitch

For this stitch, use a milliners needle in a size 3 or 5, depending on the size of the thread. Refer to Fly Stitch (page 118) and Bullion Knot (page 101) as needed.

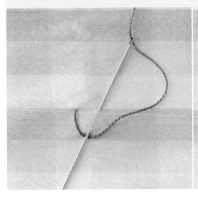 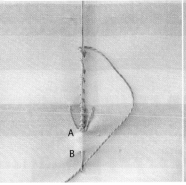 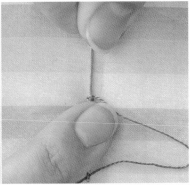

1. Bring the needle to the front of the fabric. Move the needle to the right; then slide it under the fabric at an angle. Make sure the thread is *under* the needle, as shown.

2. Pull the needle out from the fabric, and take a stitch about ¼˝ (6mm) to B. Push the tip of the needle to come out at A again, but make sure not to pull the needle through the fabric. Make sure the needle is inside the loop that was formed in Step 1. Hold the base of the needle and fabric in your left hand, pushing the tip of the needle up and away from the fabric. Pick up the thread coming out at A with your right hand. Wrap the thread around the tip of the needle in a clockwise direction. The wraps around the needle need to be at least equal to the space between A and B.

3. When you have enough wraps on the needle, cover and hold the wraps with your left thumb. Pull the needle through the wraps with your right hand, pulling the thread in an upward motion until the bullion wraps are nearly down to the fabric.

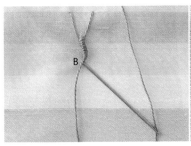 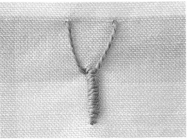

4. Pull the needle and thread toward B, laying the wraps flat against the fabric until there is no slack in the thread. Straighten any wraps that need straightening by rubbing your finger over them until they lie smooth. Push the needle and thread to the back of the fabric at B.

Bullion Knot/Lazy Daisy Combination Stitch

For this stitch, use a milliners needle in a size 3 or 5, depending on the size of the thread. Refer to Bullion Knot (page 101) and Lazy Daisy (page 122) as needed.

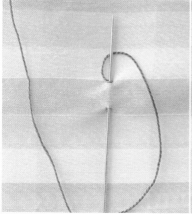

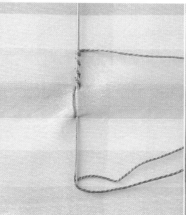

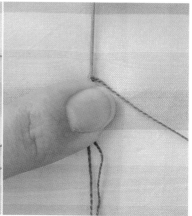

1. Bring up the needle on the edge of the stripe or crazy quilt seam, and take a stitch to the back of the fabric using the same hole, sliding the needle under the fabric. Make sure the thread is *under* the needle as it emerges from the fabric.

2. Wrap the thread around the tip of the needle in a clockwise direction 4 times.

3. When you have enough wraps on the needle, cover and hold the wraps with your left thumb. Pull the needle through the wraps with your right hand, pulling the thread in an upward motion until the bullion wraps are nearly down to the fabric.

4. Take the needle to the back of the fabric, directly beneath where the thread emerges from the bullion knot that was just completed.

Chain Stitch

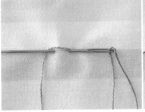  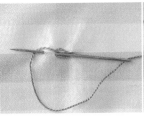 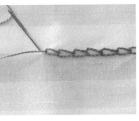

1. Bring up the needle on the edge of the stripe or crazy quilt seam, and take a stitch to the back of the fabric using the same hole, sliding the needle under the fabric.

2. Pull the thread to the front of the fabric, making sure it is *under* the needle, until the stitch forms a loop. You can control the shape of this loop by the amount of tension you have on the thread.

3. Take a stitch to the back of the fabric where the thread emerged from the last stitch, using the same hole and sliding the needle under the fabric. Repeat Step 2 until a loop forms.

4. Continue as needed. To end the stitch, take the needle to the back of the fabric just on the other side of the thread that formed the last loop.

Chain Stitch—Feathered

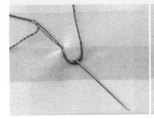   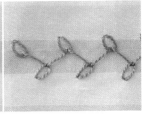

1. Bring up the needle on the upper edge of the stripe or crazy quilt seam, and take a stitch to the back of the fabric using the same hole, sliding the needle under the fabric at an angle.

2. Pull the thread to the front of the fabric, making sure the thread is *under* the needle, until the stitch forms a loop. You can control the shape of this loop by the amount of tension you have on the thread. Take the thread to the back of the fabric approximately ¼˝ (6mm) from where the thread emerged from the fabric.

3. Bring up the needle on the lower edge of the stripe or crazy quilt seam, and take a stitch to the back of the fabric using the same hole, sliding the needle under the fabric at an angle. Have the needle reemerge from the fabric very close to where the last stitch ended, making sure the thread is *under* the needle. Repeat Step 2.

4. Repeat Steps 2 and 3 as needed. Finish the last stitch by taking the needle to the back of the fabric just on the other side of the thread that formed the last stitch in Step 2.

Chain Stitch—Open

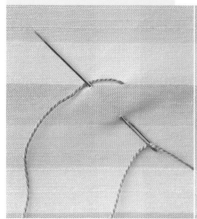
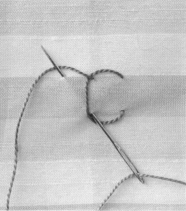
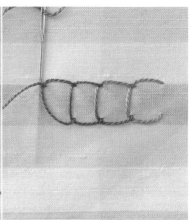

1. Bring up the needle on the lower edge of the stripe or crazy quilt seam. Below the first stitch, take a stitch at a 45° angle to the back of the fabric. Make sure that the thread is *under* the needle.

2. Pull the thread to the front of the fabric. Below where you emerged from the fabric, take a stitch at a 45° angle, making sure that the needle is inside the loop that was formed from the last stitch. Make sure that the thread is *under* the needle.

3. Repeat Step 2 as needed. To finish the stitch, take the needle to the back of the fabric just on the other side of the thread that formed the last loop. Make sure not to pull the loop too tight so that there will be enough thread to finish the loop correctly.

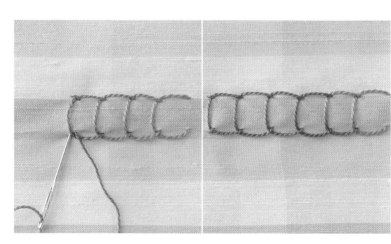

4. Bring up the needle below the last stitch, making sure that the shape of the loop looks the same as all the previous stitches. Take the needle to the back of the fabric just on the other side of the thread that formed the loop.

Chain Stitch—Open, Beaded

For demonstration purposes, I used red beading thread to make it easier to see the stitch. Normally, I use a thread that matches either the fabric or the bead, depending on the project.

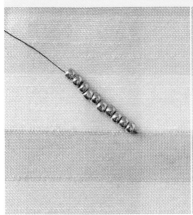 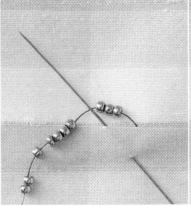 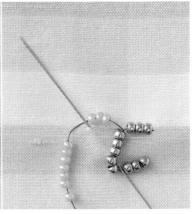

1. Bring the needle and thread up on the top edge of the stripe or crazy quilt seam. String 10 beads on the thread.

2. Take a stitch to the left at a 45° angle, making sure that 3 of the beads are to the right of the needle.

3. String 10 more beads on the thread. Take a stitch at a 45° angle from inside the loop of the first set of beads, making sure there are 3 beads to the right of the needle for both the first and second set of beads.

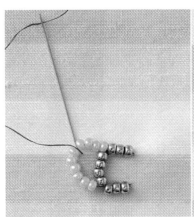  

4. Repeat Step 3 as needed. To finish the stitch, bring the needle and thread to the front of the fabric inside the loop, making sure there are 3 beads to the right of the needle. Take the needle to the back of the fabric on the other side of the thread.

5. Bring up the needle on the lower edge of the stitch inside the loop, making sure there are 3 beads to the right of the needle; then take the needle to the back of the fabric on the other side of the thread.

Chain Stitch—Two Colors

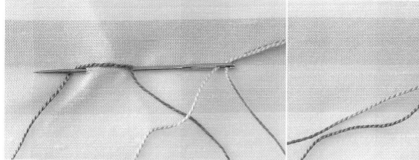 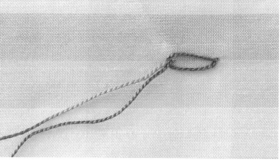

1. Thread the needle with 2 colors of thread. Bring up the needle on the edge of the stripe or crazy quilt seam, and take a stitch to the back of the fabric using the same hole, sliding the needle under the fabric. Loop one of the threads *under* the needle.

2. Pull the thread to the front of the fabric until the stitch forms a loop. You can control the shape of this loop by the amount of tension you have on the thread.

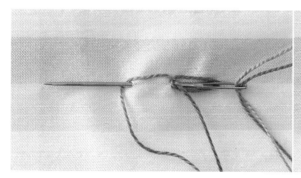 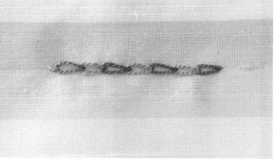

3. Take a stitch to the back of the fabric where the thread emerged from the last stitch, using the same hole and sliding the needle under the fabric. Loop the second color of thread *under* the needle, and repeat Step 2.

4. Continue as needed. To finish the stitch, take the needle to the back of the fabric just on the other side of the thread that formed the last loop.

Chevron Stitch

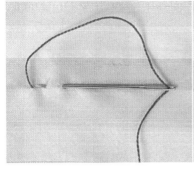 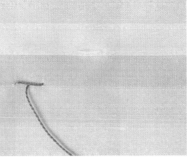 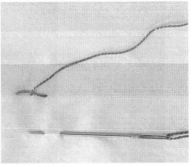

1. Bring up the needle on the edge of a stripe or crazy quilt seam, and move the needle to the right. Take a stitch to the left that is half the length of the first stitch.

2. Pull the thread to the front of the fabric, making sure the thread is centered below the stitch.

3. Move the needle to the right and down to the lower edge of the stripe or seam. Take a stitch to the left.

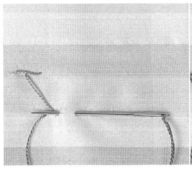 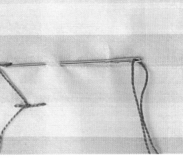 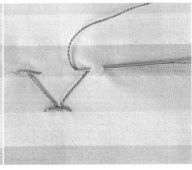

4. Pull the needle to the front of the fabric, and move the needle to the right. Take a stitch back to the left, making sure the stitch is close to the thread in the center.

5. Pull the thread to the front of the fabric, making sure the thread is centered and above the stripe or seam. Move the needle to the right and up to the top edge of the stripe or seam. Take a stitch to the right.

6. Pull the needle to the front of the fabric, and move the needle to the right, staying on the top edge of the stripe or seam. Take a stitch back to the left, making sure the stitch is close to the thread in the center.

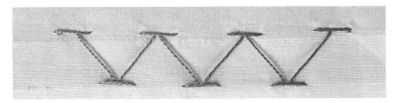

7. Continue as needed.

Chevron Stitch—Beaded

For this stitch, use a needle with an eye big enough for the thread but small enough to go through the hole of the bead. An embroidery needle usually works well for this purpose. Refer to Chevron Stitch (previous page) as needed.

1. Follow Chevron Stitch, Steps 1 and 2. String your chosen beads on the thread.

2. Take a stitch to the right, following Chevron Stitch, Steps 3 and 4. String your chosen beads on the thread.

3. Repeat Steps 1 and 2 as needed.

Chevron/Cretan Combination Stitch

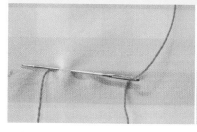 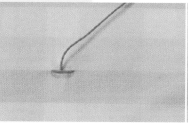 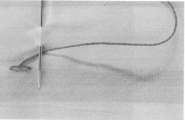

1. Bring up the needle on the edge of a stripe or crazy quilt seam, and move the needle to the right. Take a stitch to the left that is half the length of the stitch. Be sure your thread is below the needle.

2. Pull the thread to the front of the fabric, making sure the thread is centered above the stitch.

3. Move the needle to the right, and take a ¼˝ (6mm) stitch above the top stripe line. Make sure the thread is *under* the needle.

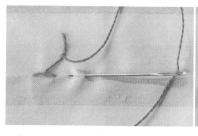 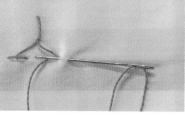 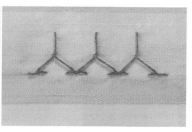

4. Move the needle to the right and down to the lower edge of the stripe or crazy quilt seam. Take a stitch to the left, making sure the thread is above the needle.

5. Pull the needle to the front of the fabric, and move the needle to the right. Take a stitch back to the left, making sure the thread is below the needle. You will also need to make sure the stitch is close to the thread in the center.

6. Repeat Steps 2–5 to continue as needed.

Chevron Stitch—Detached

When the detached version of chevron stitch is noted, it means that each stitch is done separately. In some cases, that can mean there is a space between each chevron stitch that is detached. In some examples of Chevron Stitch—Detached (page 27), there is no space between the stitches, but they are made separately.

Couching Stitch

A couching stitch is used to tack down a long straight stitch (page 126). For demonstrational purposes, I used a contrasting color of thread. If you want the couching to blend in, use the same thread you used for the straight stitch. Is it best to couch long straight stitches every ¼″–⅜″ (6–10mm).

Bring the needle to the front of the fabric on one side of the thread, and take the needle to the back of the fabric on the other side of the thread.

Tip The couching stitch will look better if you don't use the same hole that you came up from to go back down. Instead, take the thread to the back of the fabric just a thread's width away. Think of these couching stitches as small straight stitches or staples holding down the long straight stitch.

Cretan Stitch

To get a good feel for this stitch, stitch it 2 stripe widths, as demonstrated, rather than 1 stripe width.

 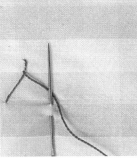 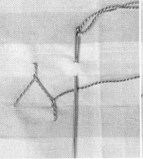 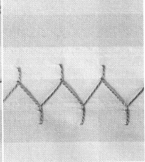

1. Bring up the needle on the middle line of the 2 stripes. (*Note:* If you are stitching on a crazy quilt seam, bring up the needle on the seam.) Move the needle to the right, and take a ¼″ (6mm) stitch above the top stripe line. Make sure the thread is *under* the needle.

2. Move the needle to the right, and take a ¼″ (6mm) stitch below the bottom stripe, making sure the thread is *under* the needle.

3. Move the needle to the right, and take a ¼″ (6mm) stitch above the top stripe, making sure the thread is *under* the needle.

4. Continue as needed.

Cretan Stitch—Beaded 1

For this stitch, use a needle with an eye big enough for the thread but small enough to go through the hole of the bead. An embroidery needle usually works well for this purpose. Refer to Cretan Stitch (page 110) as needed.

 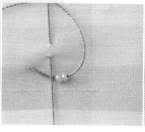 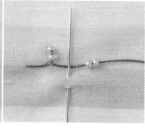 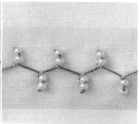

1. Pull the thread to the front of the fabric, and string 2 beads on it.

2. Follow Cretan Stitch, Step 1, keeping the 2 beads to the *right* of the needle.

3. String 2 more beads on the thread, and follow Cretan Stitch, Step 2, keeping the 2 beads to the *right* of the needle.

4. Continue as needed.

Cretan Stitch—Beaded 2

For this stitch, use a needle with an eye big enough for the thread but small enough to go through the hole of the bead. An embroidery needle usually works well for this purpose. Refer to Cretan Stitch (page 110) as needed.

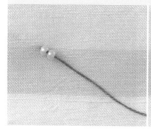 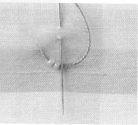 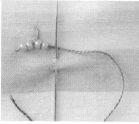 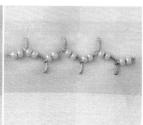

1. Pull the thread to the front of the fabric, and string 2 beads on it.

2. Follow Cretan Stitch, Step 1, keeping the 2 beads to the *left* of the needle.

3. String 2 more beads on the thread and follow Cretan Stitch, Step 2, keeping the 2 beads to the *left* of the needle.

4. Continue as needed.

Cretan Stitch—Beaded 3

For this stitch, use a needle with an eye big enough for the thread but small enough to go through the hole of the bead. An embroidery needle usually works well for this purpose. You may use one color of bead, or add interest by using 2 colors of beads. Refer to Cretan Stitch (page 110) as needed.

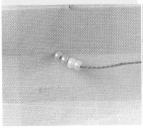 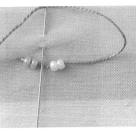 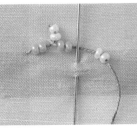 

1. Pull the thread to the front of the fabric, and string 4 beads on it.

2. Follow Cretan Stitch, Step 1, keeping 2 beads on either side of the needle.

3. String 4 more beads on the thread and follow Cretan Stitch, Step 2.

4. Continue as needed.

Cretan/Blanket Combination Stitch

See Blanket/Cretan Combination Stitch (page 100).

Cretan Stitch—Detached

Leave space between the segments, referring to the combination stitch photo for stitch placement.

Cretan/Chevron Combination Stitch

See Chevron/Cretan Combination Stitch (page 109).

Cretan/Herringbone Combination Stitch and Cretan/Herringbone Combination Stitch—Detached

See Herringbone/Cretan Combination Stitch (page 121).

Cross-Stitch

Cross-stitch is done by stitching one row of half-stitches going at a diagonal to the right and then moving back toward the left to do the second half of the stitch at a diagonal to the left.

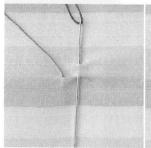 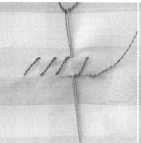 

1. Bring the needle to the front of the fabric on the lower edge of the stripe or crazy quilt seam. Take a stitch at a 45° angle to the right, taking the needle to the back of the fabric. In the same movement, bring the needle back to the front of the fabric on the lower edge of the stripe or seam.

2. Repeat Step 1 as many times as needed, moving to the right.

3. Bring the needle to the front of the fabric on the lower edge of the stripe or seam, as shown. Take a stitch at a 45° angle to the left, using the same hole that was created from the previous stitch and taking the needle to the back of the fabric. In the same movement, bring the needle to the front of the fabric on the lower edge of the stripe or seam, using the same hole from the previous stitch.

4. Continue as needed.

Detached Wheat Ear Stitch

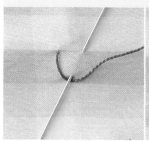 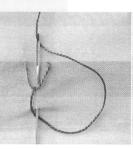 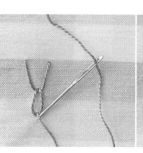

1. Bring the needle to the front of the fabric, move it to the right, then slide it under the fabric at an angle. Make sure the thread is *under* the needle.

2. Pull the thread to the front of the fabric, and take a stitch to the back of the fabric, using the same hole where the thread emerged from the fabric. Slide the needle under the fabric, and bring it to the front of the fabric below the previous stitch. Make sure the thread is *under* the needle.

3. Take the thread to the back of the fabric, stitching just on the other side of the thread that forms the loop.

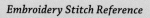

Featherstitch

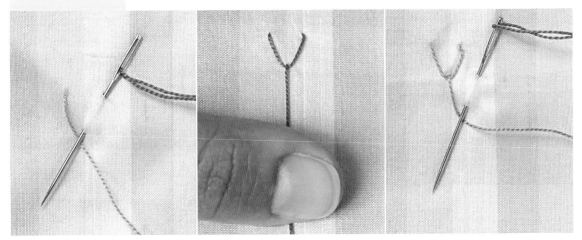

1. Bring up the needle on the left side of the stripe or crazy quilt seam. Move the needle to the right, and then slide the needle under the fabric at an angle. Make sure the thread is *under* the needle, as shown.

Tip — By varying the angle of the needle, you can make the featherstitch look completely different. Experiment with the angles, and see how many different featherstitches you can make.

2. Pull the needle out from the fabric, and gently pull the thread up and then down. Hold it in place with your left thumb.

3. Move the needle to the right, and repeat Step 1.

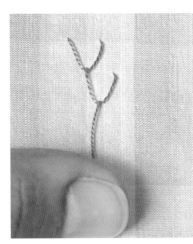

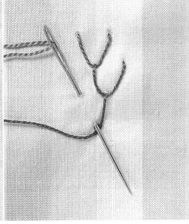

4. Pull the needle out from the fabric, and gently pull the thread up and then down, as you did in Step 2.

5. Move the needle to the left, and repeat Step 1.

6. Continue as needed.

Featherstitch—Double

This stitch is very similar to a basic featherstitch. The only difference is the direction that you move the needle and thread.

1. Follow Featherstitch, Steps 1–4 (page 114).

2. Move the needle to the right, and repeat Featherstitch, Step 1.

3. Move the needle to the left, and repeat Featherstitch, Step 1. Repeat this step again, moving the needle to the left.

4. Continue as needed.

Featherstitch—Double, Beaded

For demonstrational purposes, I used red beading thread to make it easier to see the stitch. Normally, I use a thread that matches either the fabric or the bead, depending on the project. Also for demonstrational purposes, I used a pen to mark my lines. Normally, I use a purple air-erasable pen that fades away after I finish stitching.

1. Draw a ¼˝ (6mm) line on either side of the striped fabric or crazy quilt seam. Bring the needle and thread to the front of the fabric on the lower edge of the drawn line, and string 7 beads on the thread.

2. Take the needle to the back of the fabric on the stripe or seamline.

3. Bring the needle and thread to the front of the fabric, coming up close to where the middle (fourth) bead on the string sits when it lies flat on the fabric. Move the needle in an *upward* direction, and slide it through the middle bead. Pull the needle out of the middle bead, and string 7 more beads on the thread.

Continued on next page

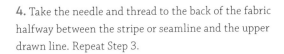

4. Take the needle and thread to the back of the fabric halfway between the stripe or seamline and the upper drawn line. Repeat Step 3.

5. String 7 more beads on the thread, and take the needle and thread to the back of the fabric on the edge of the upper line. Bring the needle and thread to the front of the fabric, coming up close to where the middle bead on the string sits when it lies flat on the fabric. Move the needle in a *downward* direction, and slide it through the middle bead. Pull the needle out of the middle bead, and string 7 more beads on the thread.

6. Take the needle to the back of the fabric halfway between the stripe or seamline and the lower drawn line. Bring the needle and thread to the front of the fabric, coming up close to where the middle bead on the string sits when it lies flat on the fabric. Move the needle in a *downward* direction, and slide it through the middle bead. Pull the needle out of the middle bead, and string 7 more beads on the thread.

7. Take the needle and thread to the back of the fabric on the edge of the lower stripe. To finish the stitch, bring the needle and thread to the front of the fabric, coming up close to where the middle bead on the string sits when it lies flat on the fabric. Move the needle in an *upward* direction, and slide it through the middle bead. Pull the needle out of the middle bead, and take the needle to the back of the fabric on the other side of the bead. To continue the stitch, string 7 beads on the thread and repeat Steps 4–7 as needed.

Featherstitch—Triple

This stitch is very similar to a basic featherstitch. The only difference is the direction that you move the needle and thread.

1. Follow Featherstitch, Steps 1–4 (page 114).

2. Move the needle to the right, and repeat Featherstitch, Step 1.

3. Move the needle to the right again. Repeat Featherstitch, Step 1.

4. Move the needle to the left, and repeat Featherstitch, Step 1. Repeat this step 2 more times, moving the needle to the left.

5. Continue as needed.

Featherstitch—Knotted

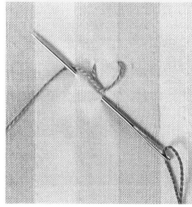 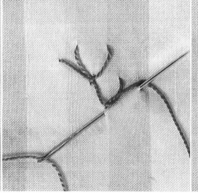 

1. Follow Featherstitch, Steps 1 and 2 (page 114), and then take a stitch that starts at the base of the featherstitch and angles outward. Loop the thread around the needle, as shown, and pull the needle toward you until the stitch lies flat on the fabric.

2. Follow Featherstitch, Steps 3 and 4; then repeat Step 1 (at left), looping the thread around the needle as shown.

3. Continue as needed.

Fly Stitch   This stitch is also called the *Y-stitch*.

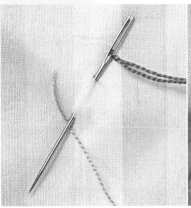 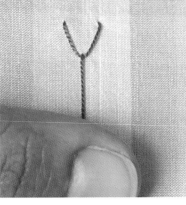 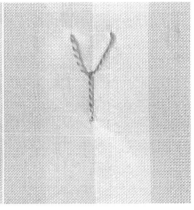

1. Bring up the needle to the left of the stripe or crazy quilt seam. Move the needle to the right, and then slide it under the fabric at an angle. Make sure the thread is *under* the needle, as shown.

2. Pull the needle out from the fabric, and gently pull the thread up and then down. Hold it in place with your left thumb.

3. Take the thread to the back of the fabric.

Fly Stitch—Beaded

For demonstrational purposes, I used red beading thread to make it easier to see the stitch. Normally, I use a thread that matches either the fabric or the bead, depending on the project.

1. Bring up the needle on the edge of a stripe or crazy quilt seam, and string 6 beads on the thread.

2. Move the needle ¼″ (6mm) to the right, and take it to the back of the fabric.

3. Bring up the needle just inside the loop that was formed in Step 2, with 3 beads on each side, making sure that a V is formed and the beads lie flat on the fabric.

4. String 4 beads on the thread.

5. Take the needle to the back of the fabric, making sure the beads lie flat on the fabric.

Fly Stitch/Bullion Knot Combination Stitch

See Bullion Knot/Fly Stitch Combination Stitch (page 102).

French Knot

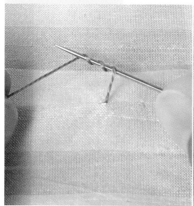 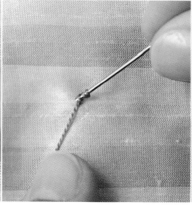 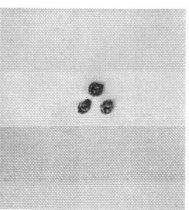

1. Bring the needle to the front of the fabric. Holding the needle in your right hand, take the thread in your left hand and bring it in front of the needle. Wrap the thread twice around the needle.

2. Take the needle to the back of the fabric close to where you came up, holding the thread in your left hand. Pull the thread until the French knot is snug against the fabric.

Herringbone Stitch

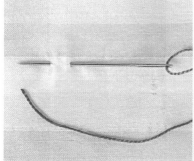 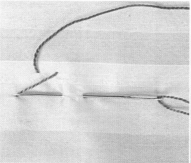 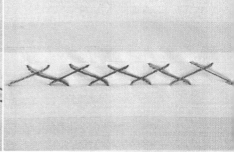

1. Bring up the needle on the lower edge of the striped fabric or crazy quilt seam. Move the needle to the right, and take a stitch on the upper edge of the stripe or seam. Make sure the thread is placed *below* the needle.

2. Pull the thread out from the fabric. Move the needle to the right, and take a stitch on the lower edge of the stripe or seam in the same manner as before. Make sure the thread is placed *above* the needle.

3. Continue as needed.

Herringbone Stitch—Backstitched

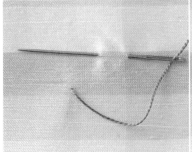 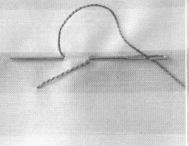 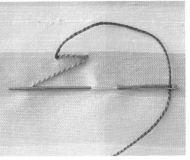

1. Bring up the needle on the lower edge of the striped fabric or crazy quilt seam. Move the needle to the right, and take a stitch on the upper edge of the stripe or seam. Make sure the thread is placed *below* the needle.

2. Pull the thread to the front of the fabric, and move the needle back to the right. Take a stitch going into the same hole where the thread went to the back of the fabric. Slide the needle under the fabric, moving to the left, and reemerge in the same hole where the thread came out of the fabric. Make sure to keep the thread placed *above* the needle while doing this part of the stitch.

3. Pull the thread out from the fabric. Move the needle to the right, and take a stitch on the lower edge of the stripe or seam in the same manner as before. Make sure that the thread is placed *above* the needle.

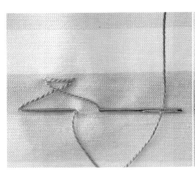 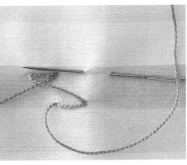 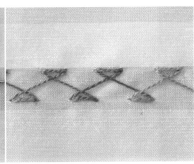

4. Pull the thread to the front of the fabric, and move the needle back to the right. Take a stitch going into the same hole where the thread went to the back of the fabric. Slide the needle under the fabric, moving to the left, and reemerge in the same hole where the thread came out of the fabric. Make sure to keep the thread placed *below* the needle while doing this part of the stitch.

5. Pull the needle to the front of the fabric, and repeat Step 2.

6. Continue as needed.

Herringbone/Blanket Combination Stitch

Refer to Herringbone Stitch (page 119) and Blanket Stitch (page 95) as needed.

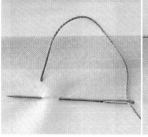 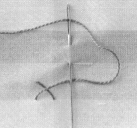 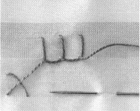 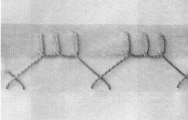

1. Bring the needle to the front of the fabric in the middle of the lower stripe. Move the needle to the right, and take a stitch back to the left on the lower edge of the stripe. The needle should reemerge directly below where the thread came out of the fabric. Make sure the thread is placed *above* the needle. Pull the needle to the front of the fabric.

2. Move the needle to the right, and place the needle in a perpendicular position, moving in a downward direction. Make sure the thread is placed *under* the needle. Pull the needle to the front of the fabric.

3. Repeat Step 2 twice. Move the needle to the right, and take a stitch back to the left on the lower edge of the stripe. Make sure the thread is placed *above* the needle. Pull the needle to the front of the fabric.

4. Repeat Steps 2 and 3 as needed.

Herringbone/Cretan Combination Stitch

Refer to Herringbone Stitch (page 119) and Cretan Stitch (page 110) as needed.

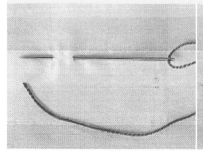  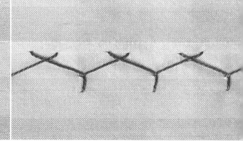

1. Bring up the needle on the lower edge of the striped fabric or crazy quilt seam. Move the needle to the right, and take a stitch that is parallel to the upper edge of the stripe or seam and moves from right to left. Make sure the thread is placed *below* the needle.

2. Move the needle to the right, and take a stitch below the lower edge of the stripe or seam, making sure the thread is *under* the needle.

3. Move the needle to the right, and repeat Step 1.

4. Continue as needed.

Herringbone/Cretan Combination Stitch—Detached

Leave space between the segments, referring to the stitch-combination photos for placement.

Herringbone Stitch—Detached

Leave space between the segments, referring to the stitch-combination photos for placement.

Lazy Daisy

This stitch is also called the *detached chain stitch*.

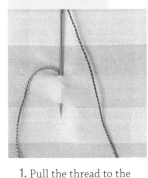
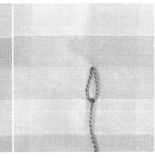

1. Pull the thread to the front of the fabric on the edge of the stripe or seam, and take a stitch to the back of the fabric using the same hole where the thread emerged from the fabric. Slide the needle under the fabric and bring it to the front of the fabric, below the previous stitch. Make sure the thread is *under* the needle.

2. Pull the thread to the front of the fabric.

3. Pull on the thread until the stitch forms a loop. You can control the shape of this loop by the amount of tension you have on the thread.

4. Take the thread to the back of the fabric, stitching just on the other side of the thread that forms the loop.

Lazy Daisy/Bullion Knot Combination Stitch

See Bullion Knot/Lazy Daisy Combination Stitch (page 103).

Maidenhair Stitch

Follow the steps of Featherstitch (page 114), but alter the placement of the individual stitches to match the photos of the Maidenhair Stitch.

Pistil Stitch This stitch incorporates a French knot. Refer to French Knot (page 119) as needed.

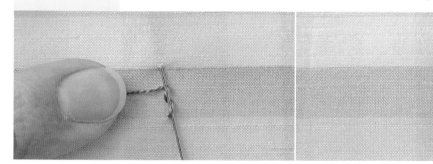

Pull the thread to the front of the fabric. Wrap the thread around the needle twice, and take it to the back of the fabric ⅜″ (10mm) from where the thread emerged from the fabric. While holding the thread with your left thumb, pull the thread until the French knot is snug against the fabric.

Rosette Stitch

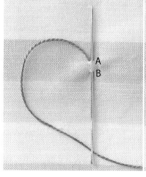 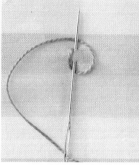 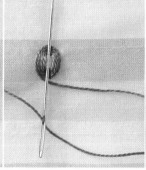 

1. Pull the needle and thread to the front of the fabric at A. Take a stitch about ¼″ (6mm) to B, and push the tip of the needle to come out at A again, making sure not to pull the needle through the fabric.

2. Wrap the thread around the needle in a counterclockwise direction under the needle.

3. Wrap the thread around the needle 4 times, and end with the thread on the right side of the needle on the lower end of the stitch.

4. Hold the wraps with your left thumb, and pull the needle through the wraps with your right hand.

Continued on next page

5. Take the needle to the back of the fabric just on the other side of the outside edge of the wraps. *Make sure not to pull too tightly—you want to leave the loop that has formed on the bottom of the wraps in place.*

6. Bring up the needle through the inside of the loops on the bottom of the wraps. Take the needle to the back of the fabric on the other side of the loops.

Running Stitch

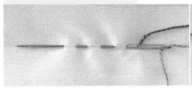 

1. Pull the thread to the front of the fabric, and move the needle in and out of the fabric at equal distances.

2. Pull the thread to the front of the fabric, and repeat Step 1 as needed.

Sheaf Stitch

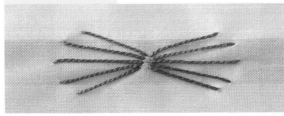 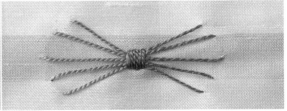

1. Pull the needle and thread to the front of the fabric, and make a series of angled horizontal straight stitches, as shown.

2. Make a series of vertical straight stitches close together to fill in the space between the 2 sets of horizontal straight stitches.

Star Stitch

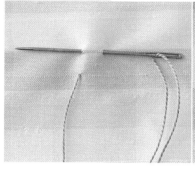 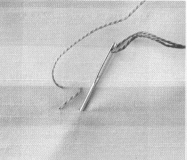 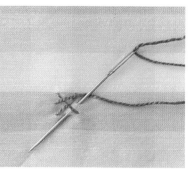

1. Bring the needle to the front of the fabric, and take a stitch at a 45° angle to the right, taking the needle to the back of the fabric. In the same movement, going to the left, bring the needle back to the front of the fabric on the top edge of the stripe or crazy quilt seam.

2. Pull the needle to the front of the fabric, and take a stitch at a 45° angle to the right, taking the needle to the back of the fabric.

3. Bring the needle to the front of the fabric on the left side of the stitch, and take a stitch to the right, taking the needle to the back of the fabric. In the same movement, angle the needle to the lower edge of the stitch, bringing the needle to the front of the fabric.

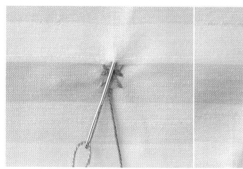 

4. Pull the needle to the front of the fabric, and take a stitch on the top edge of the stripe or seam, as shown. Take the needle to the back of the fabric.

Stem Stitch

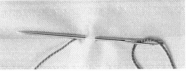  

1. Bring up the needle on the edge of the stripe or crazy quilt seam. Move the needle to the right, and take a stitch to the left, making sure to keep the thread placed *below* the needle.

2. Pull the needle to the front of the fabric, and move the needle to the right. Take a stitch to the left, keeping the thread placed *below* the needle, and come up close to the last stitch that you made.

3. Repeat Step 2 as needed.

Stem Stitch—Beaded

For demonstrational purposes, I used red beading thread to make it easier to see the stitch. Normally, I use a thread that matches either the fabric or the bead, depending on the project.

1. Bring up the needle on the edge of the stripe or crazy quilt seam, and string 6 beads on the thread.

2. Take the needle to the back of the fabric, making sure the beads lie flat on the fabric. Bring the needle back up on the edge of the same stripe or seam, counting back 2 beads.

3. String 6 more beads on the thread, and repeat Step 2.

4. Continue as needed. To give the stitch a more finished look, add 2 beads on the end of the upper right side and 2 beads on the end of the lower left side.

Straight Stitch

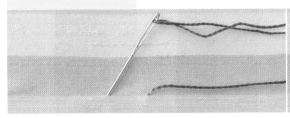 

1. Pull the needle to the front of the fabric, and move the needle over the distance needed to complete the stitch.

2. Take the stitch to the back of the fabric.

Silk Ribbon Embroidery Stitches

THREADING AND KNOTTING SILK RIBBON

Embroidering with silk ribbon is a little bit different than with thread. One big difference is the way you thread the needle and tie the knot on the end. For silk ribbon embroidery, it is best to use a #22 or #24 chenille needle. You may use silk ribbon to do regular embroidery stitches, but keep in mind that you should use less tension when pulling on the stitch so that the ribbon will look soft and full.

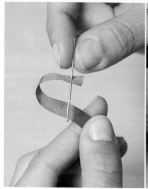 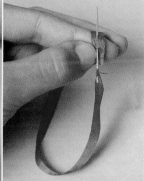  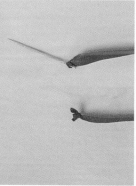

1. Thread the silk ribbon through the eye of the needle. Take the end of the ribbon and pierce it with the needle about ¼″ (6mm) from the raw edge.

2. To knot the end of the ribbon, grab the lower raw edge between your thumb and forefinger. Wrap the ribbon away from you around your forefinger. Take a stitch through the ribbon on your finger about ¼″ (6mm) from the raw edge.

3. Pull the ribbon down over the eye of the needle and continue moving it down the length of the ribbon until a knot forms.

Silk ribbon after being threaded and knotted correctly

Chain Stitch Rose

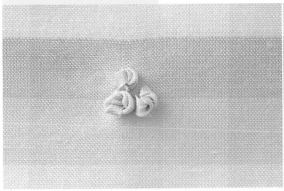 

1. Embroider 3 French knots (page 119) with silk ribbon to make a center for the rose.

2. Bring the needle to the front of the fabric, close to the 3 French knots. Stitch a chain stitch (page 104) in silk ribbon, working in a counterclockwise direction around the center French knots. Continue to chain-stitch, spiraling out until the rose is the desired size.

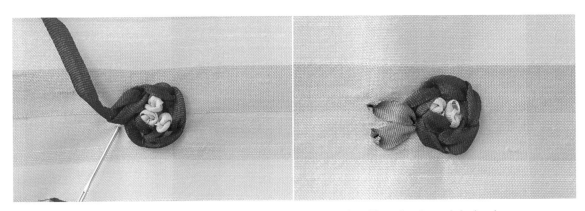

3. Take the needle to the back of the fabric just on the other side of the ribbon that formed the last loop.

Colonial Knot

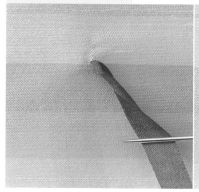 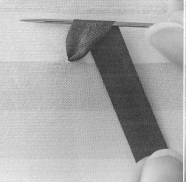 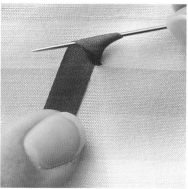

1. Bring the ribbon to the front of the fabric. While holding the ribbon in your left hand, place the needle perpendicular to the fabric on the left-hand side of the ribbon. Notice how the ribbon is flat while this stitch is made.

2. While holding the needle in the perpendicular position and still holding the ribbon in your left hand, rotate the needle in a counterclockwise motion until the needle is in a horizontal position, as shown.

3. Wrap the ribbon that is in your left hand around the needle once, moving from the top to the bottom. *Keep the tension in the ribbon loose to make a softer-looking Colonial knot.*

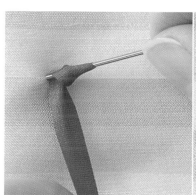 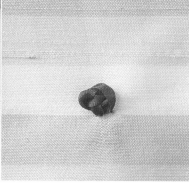

4. Take the ribbon to the back of the fabric, close to where the ribbon came up, without catching the knot on the back of the fabric. *Make sure not to pull too tightly or the Colonial knot will become very small.*

Colonial Knot Running Stitch Rose

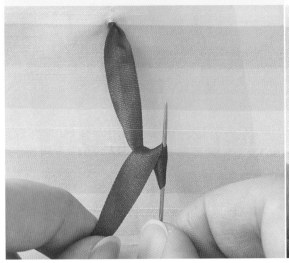

1. Pull the ribbon to the front of the fabric. Follow Colonial Knot, Steps 1–3 (page 129) using silk ribbon, leaving 1½″ (3.8cm) of ribbon between the fabric and the in-progress Colonial knot.

2. Make a running stitch along the length of the ribbon left between the fabric and the Colonial knot, moving the needle back and forth in a zigzag motion from the left edge to the right edge of the ribbon. This will make the rose look fuller.

Tip The smaller you make the running stitch, the smaller the rose will be, and vice versa.

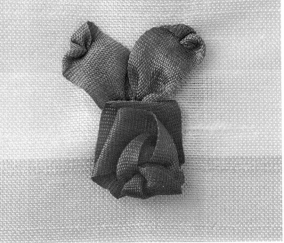

3. After completing the running stitch along the length of the ribbon, take the needle to the back of the fabric. *Make sure not to pull too tightly or the rose won't look as full and natural.*

Loop Flower

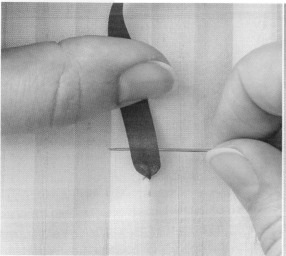

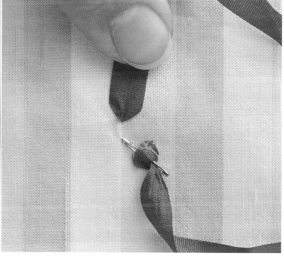

1. Bring the needle to the front of the fabric. Place the needle under the ribbon and, with slight pressure, move it toward the fabric. This helps smooth out any wrinkles in the ribbon.

2. Take the needle to the back of the fabric, just below the first stitch.

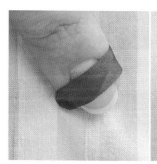

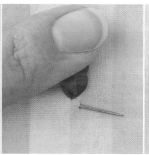

3. Pull the ribbon to the back of the fabric, keeping your index finger in the ribbon until the loop is the desired size.

4. Working in a clockwise direction, repeat Steps 1–3 to make a flower. *Make sure to pull gently or the already stitched loops will pull through and will need to be stitched again.*

5. Make a French knot (page 119) in silk ribbon in the center.

Plume Stitch

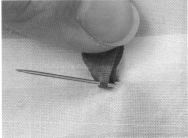
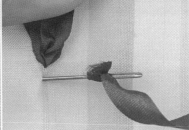

1. Follow Loop Flower, Steps 1–3 (page 131).

2. Hold the loop in place, and pierce the lower edge of the previous stitch before bringing the needle to the front of the fabric.

3. Take the needle to the back of the fabric, just below the last stitch. While pulling, keep your index finger in the ribbon until the loop is the desired size, as in Loop Flower, Step 3.

4. Repeat Steps 2 and 3 to complete the desired number of loops. Pull the last loop flat.

Ribbon Stitch

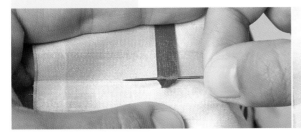

1. Bring the needle to the front of the fabric. Place the needle under the ribbon and, with slight pressure, move it toward the fabric. This helps smooth out any wrinkles in the ribbon.

Tip You may make this stitch any length to fit the project you are working on. To give the stitch a more natural look, ease some of the tension in the ribbon before piercing it with the needle.

2. With the needle, pierce the middle of the ribbon about ½″ (1.2cm) from where it came out of the fabric. Pierce into the fabric as well.

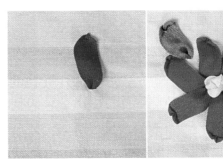

3. Pull the needle to the back of the fabric until the ribbon comes to a point. Repeat Steps 1–3 to make a flower and leaves. Make a French knot (page 119) in silk ribbon in the center.

Side Ribbon Stitch Flower

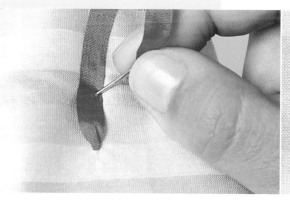

1. Follow Ribbon Stitch, Step 1 (page 132).

2. Pierce the right edge of the ribbon with the needle.

3. Gently pull the needle to the back of the fabric until the ribbon comes to a point.

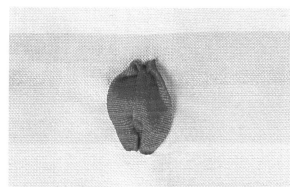

4. Bring the ribbon up on the right side of the first stitch you made. Pierce the *left* edge of the ribbon with the needle. Gently pull the needle to the back of the fabric until the ribbon comes to a point. Repeat Steps 1–3 to make a flower and leaves. Make a French knot (page 119) in the center.

Spider Web Rose

For demonstrational purposes, I used a pen to mark my circle. Normally, I use a purple air-erasable pen that fades away after I finish stitching.

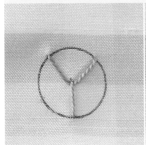   

1. Draw a circle on the fabric and mark the center. Stitch a Fly Stitch (page 118) in thread, using the center mark as a guide.

2. Stitch 2 straight stitches (page 126) in thread on either side of the fly stitch, taking the needle from the outside line and going to the back of the fabric in the center of the circle for each stitch. Make sure the stitches are evenly placed around the circle. You should end up with 5 spokes as a foundation for the rose.

3. Switching to a needle that has been threaded with silk ribbon, bring the needle to the front of the fabric very close to the center.

4. In a counterclockwise direction, weave the ribbon over and under the spokes to complete the first round.

5. After completing the first round, pull the ribbon snug against the center threads so they won't show.

6. Continue in a counterclockwise direction, weaving the ribbon over and under the spokes until the threads are no longer visible. Use less tension on the ribbon to give the rose some fullness. Take the ribbon to the back of the fabric just under the ribbon.

Stem Stitch Rose

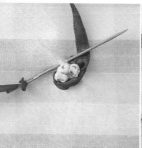

1. Embroider 3 French knots (page 119) with silk ribbon to make a center for the rose.

2. Bring the needle to the front of the fabric, close to the 3 French knots. Stitch a stem stitch (page 126) in silk ribbon, working in a counterclockwise direction near the center French knots. Continue to make stem stitches, spiraling out until the rose is the desired size.

3. Take the ribbon to the back of the fabric just under the ribbon.

Straight Stitch Flower

Bring the needle to the front of the fabric, and take a stitch ¼" (6mm) away, leaving the ribbon loose. Repeat to make a flower and leaves. Make a French knot (page 119) in the center.

Background Piecing Basics

Rainbow Sampler

Foundation-Piecing Tutorial

A few years ago, I ordered a full line of Tula Pink Solids because I thought the colors were so stunning. I loved the way the fabrics emulated the colors in the rainbow and decided that they would be perfect in some type of sampler. This foundation strip-piecing method was a fun and different way to make a sampler. I made the sampler narrow so that I could try as many stitch combinations as possible in a short amount of time.

I had so much fun doing this sampler that I made a second one, the *Pansy Sampler* (page 76), in my favorite pastels. You can make this sampler in any color combination that pleases you—the combinations are limitless!

FINISHED SAMPLER:

5½″ × 34″ (14 × 86.4cm)

Materials

MUSLIN: 5½″ × 34″
(14 × 86.4cm)

ASSORTED SOLIDS:
22 solids cut into 2″ × 5½″
(14 × 86.4cm) strips (These can be 22 different colors, or you may repeat some of the colors.)

FINE-POINT PERMANENT MARKER (I used a Sharpie.)

Piecing the Sampler Background

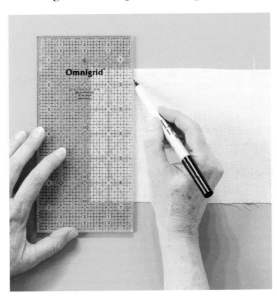

1. Using the marker and a clear ruler, begin by drawing the design on the 5½″ × 34″ (14 × 86.4cm) muslin foundation. Starting on the left end of the muslin, draw a line 1¾″ (4.4cm) away from the edge and perpendicular to the long edge of the muslin.

3. Continue moving down the muslin strip, drawing a line every 1½″ (3.8cm). When you reach the end of the muslin, the final line should be 1¾″ (4.4cm) away from the raw edge. Both lines drawn on the ends are 1¾″(4.4cm) away from the raw edge to allow enough room for a seam allowance. You should have a total of 21 lines.

Tip You could make your sampler longer or shorter if you would like. Make your muslin foundation 1½″ (3.8cm) longer for each strip you add or 1½″ (3.8cm) shorter for each strip you subtract. You may also change the width of your sampler by cutting your muslin foundation to the width that you would like.

2. Move to the right and draw another line that is 1½″ (3.8cm) away from the last line, still making it perpendicular to the long edge.

4. Lay the muslin down with the unmarked side facing up. Place the first 2″ × 5½″ (5.1 × 14cm) strip of fabric on top of the muslin, making sure it is lined up with the raw edge. You may start working from the left or right edge.

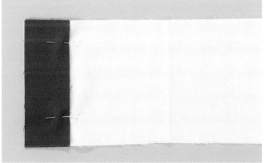

5. Place the next 2″ × 5½″ (5.1 × 14cm) fabric strip on top of the first one, and pin in place through all 3 layers.

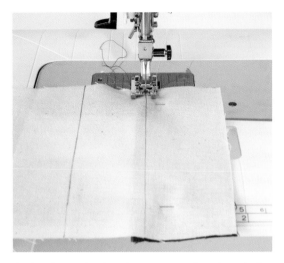

6. Flip the muslin foundation over to the side with the drawn line. Sew through all 3 layers on the line.

7. Trim the seam to ⅛″ (3mm). Flip the fabric to the right side and press.

Tip Trimming the seam to ⅛″ (3mm) makes it easier to embroider. When the seam is thick, it is harder to get the needle through the fabric and the stitches won't lie as flat on the fabric.

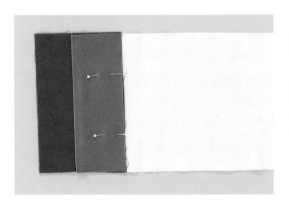

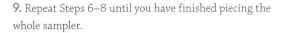

8. Place the next 2″ × 5½″ (5.1 × 14cm) fabric strip on top of the second one that you just sewed and pin through all 3 layers.

9. Repeat Steps 6–8 until you have finished piecing the whole sampler.

10. Pin the last piece you stitched into place. Working from the wrong (or muslin) side of the rectangle, sew around the perimeter of the block ⅛″ (3mm) from the edge.

Crazy Quilt Piecing

Many of the samplers that I made for this book were done using the Montano Centerpiece Method, but the Montano Fan Method would also be a good option for changing the look of your sampler. When deciding how big to make your block, I suggest measuring your hoop and adding 4″ (10.2cm) to that measurement. That will give you enough extra fabric to be able to finish the hoop when you are done.

Montano Centerpiece Method

1. Cut a 5-sided fabric shape, and pin it right side up in the center of a square piece of muslin.

2. Cut a rectangular piece that fits on a side of the center fabric.

3. Pin the rectangular piece wrong side up, aligning it with the straight edge. Sew with an ⅛″ (3mm) seam allowance. Press open.

4. Working clockwise, cut the next piece of fabric. It should be long enough to match the edge of the rectangular piece of fabric and the next side of the 5-sided shape.

5. Pin the piece wrong side up, and sew with an ⅛″ (3mm) seam allowance. Trim the excess fabric from the seam and press open.

Tip To make the block more interesting, start cutting different fabric shapes other than the rectangular shape you started with.

6. Repeat Steps 2–5 for the third, fourth, and fifth sides of the 5-sided shape.

7. Continue working clockwise until you have completely covered the muslin.

Tip It is always a good idea to repeat some fabrics a couple of times in a block. Strategically place them so that the block looks balanced.

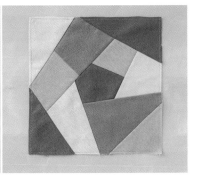

8. Trim the outside edges even with the muslin square. Working from the wrong (or muslin) side of the square, sew around the perimeter of the block ⅛″ (3mm) from the edge. This keeps the outer edges of the fabric in place.

Tip You can give a block a "crazier" look by sewing together 2 pieces of fabric and then treating them as 1 piece when you sew them in place.

Montano Fan Method

1. Cut a 5-sided fabric shape with a 90° corner. Pin it right side up to the upper left corner of a square piece of muslin.

2. Working clockwise, cut a rectangular piece that fits on the top right raw edge of the 5-sided shape. Pin the rectangular piece wrong side up, aligning it with the straight edge of the 5-sided shape. Sew with an ⅛″ (3mm) seam allowance. Press open.

Tip To make the block more interesting, start cutting different fabric shapes other than the rectangular shape you started with.

3. Cut a third piece of fabric. It should be long enough to cover the previous rectangular piece of fabric and align with the next side of the 5-sided shape. Some of the rectangle will extend beyond this new piece and will be trimmed later. Pin the piece wrong side up and sew with an ⅛″ (3mm) seam allowance. Trim the excess fabric from the seam of the previous piece, and press open.

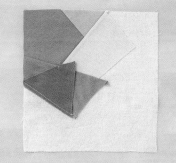

4. Cut a fourth piece of fabric long enough to cover the bottom edge of the first corner piece. Pin into place on the right edge, and sew with an ⅛″ (3mm) seam allowance. Trim the excess fabric from the seam and press open.

5. Working *counterclockwise*, cut a piece of fabric to cover part of the bottom edge of the piece you attached in Step 4. Pin in place, and sew with an ⅛″ (3mm) seam allowance. Trim the excess fabric from the seam and press open.

6. Cut another piece of fabric long enough to cover most of the bottom edges of the last 2 pieces that you added. Pin in place, and sew with an ⅛″ (3mm) seam allowance. Trim the excess fabric from the seam and press open.

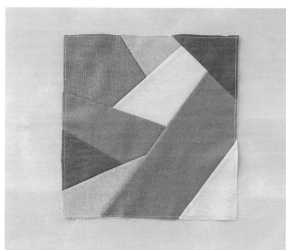
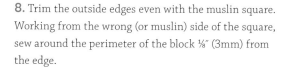
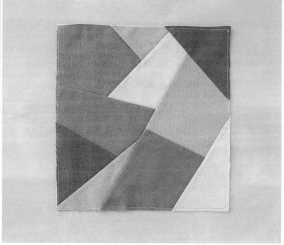

7. Continue piecing the block counterclockwise until you reach the right edge of the muslin square. When you reach the edge, begin to work *clockwise* until you have covered the muslin.

8. Trim the outside edges even with the muslin square. Working from the wrong (or muslin) side of the square, sew around the perimeter of the block ⅛″ (3mm) from the edge.

Tip You can give a block a "crazier" look by sewing together 2 pieces of fabric and then treating them as 1 piece when you sew them in place.

Stitch Patterns

For Bullion Knot rose + Straight Stitch + French Knot + Seed Beads (pages 21, 22, 35, 62, and 66), do 9 wraps for the 2 center Bullion Knots and 12 wraps for each of the outer Bullion Knots.

For Bullion Knot rose + Lazy Daisy + Straight Stitch + Seed Beads (page 22), do 12 wraps for the center 4 Bullion Knots, 25 wraps for the 4 Bullion Knots in the second layer, and 27 wraps for the 4 Bullion Knots in the outer layer of the rose.

About the Author

Photo by Jacob Bothell

Valerie Bothell has happily taught crazy quilting for more than twenty years and has enjoyed every minute of it. She is the coauthor of *Quilting ... Just a Little Bit Crazy* and the author of *Joyful Daily Stitching*. Traveling and teaching are very rewarding for her, and she always looks forward to every opportunity to share her love of crazy quilting.

Valerie has been married for 28 years and has 4 very handsome sons. When she is not crazy quilting, she loves to go to the beach, read books, and ride her bike with her sweet dog, Daisy. She also enjoys giving Quilts of Valor to veterans who have served or are currently serving in the military. As a proud member of the Daughters of the American Revolution, she also enjoys making quilts that have historical significance.

ALSO BY VALERIE BOTHELL: